W9-AVH-346

Compass of the Soul

Other Books by Lynn A. Robinson

Divine Intuition:
Your Guide to Creating a Life You Love

With Lavonne Carlson Finnerty
The Complete Idiot's Guide to Being Psychic

COMPASS
OF THE
SOUL

52 WAYS INTUITION CAN GUIDE YOU TO THE LIFE OF YOUR DREAMS

LYNN A. ROBINSON

**Andrews McMeel
Publishing**

Kansas City

Compass of the Soul copyright © 2003 by Lynn A. Robinson.
All rights reserved. Printed in the United States of America.
No part of this book may be used or reproduced in any manner
whatsoever without written permission except in the case
of reprints in the context of reviews. For information, write
Andrews McMeel Publishing, an Andrews McMeel Universal
company, 4520 Main Street, Kansas City, Missouri 64111.

04 05 06 07 MLT 10 9 8 7 6 5 4 3 2

Library of Congress Cataloging-in-Publication Data
Robinson, Lynn A.
    Compass of the soul : 52 ways intuition can guide you to the life
of your dreams / Lynn A. Robinson.
        p. cm.
    ISBN 0-7407-3337-0 (pbk.)
    1. Intuition—Problems, exercises, etc. 2. Intuition. I. Title.
BF315.5 .R63 2003
153.4'4—dc21
                                                                2002028287

Book design and composition by
Kelly & Company, Lee's Summit, Missouri

———————— ATTENTION: SCHOOLS AND BUSINESSES ————————

Andrews McMeel books are available at quantity discounts with
bulk purchase for educational, business, or sales promotional use.
For information, please write to: Special Sales Department, Andrews
McMeel Publishing, 4520 Main Street, Kansas City, Missouri 64111.

ACKNOWLEDGMENTS

A good book is a product of collaboration, so I consider myself fortunate to have had a wealth of support in creating *Compass of the Soul*. Much gratitude and appreciation to:

❋ My wonderful agent, John Willig, who can always find a ray of light in any situation. Thanks for your support, patience, determination, and great sense of humor.

❋ Jean Lucas, my editor—thank you for being so vigilant in your pursuit to add clarity and readability to my book.

❋ Shane Bowlin, my virtual assistant extraordinaire. I wouldn't have gotten this far in my career without you. You pick me up when I'm down and make me laugh. And when all else fails, you send chocolate. You help the world know about me and my work and I'm eternally grateful.

❋ My dear friend and soul sister, Laura Straus. You always encourage me to dream big. Thanks for believing in me.

❋ My terrific friends and colleagues Bob and Gail Beck, Savita and Michael Brewer, Chrissy Carew, Mimi Doe, Michael Gerrish, Lori Hanau, Alison Hendren, John Holland, Shiri Hughes, Gail McMeekin, Nancy Michaels, Marina Petro, Jean Redpath, Cheryl Richardson, Diane Ripstein, Barbara Selwyn,

ACKNOWLEDGMENTS

Simon Steel, Mark and Beth Sullivan, and so many others.
Thank you for being there.

✳ My stepson, Cliff. I'm so proud of you. I wish you many blessings as you continue on your path to creating a life you love.

✳ My husband, Gary. I feel so blessed by your love and support.
Life wouldn't be nearly as much fun if it weren't for you. I am
very lucky to be married to such a wonderful, intelligent, and
kind man.

INTRODUCTION

Compass of the Soul:

52 Ways Intuition Can Guide You to the Life of Your Dreams

I am extremely grateful to the thousands of people who read my book *Divine Intuition: Your Guide to Creating a Life You Love*. Many of you took the message to heart and shared warm and wonderful stories about how it had changed your lives. I also received calls, e-mails, and letters asking me when I would be available in various areas to present this material in person. As I haven't yet mastered the ability to be in several places at the same time, I decided to write this book and share a bit of the workshop experience with all of you!

Intuition comes in many forms. It communicates in different ways to each of us. There is no one right way to hear its guidance. *Compass of the Soul* provides a chapter-by-chapter plan to enable you to create the life you've always wanted through the use of intuition. Each chapter consists of four parts:

An inspirational quote.

An intuition lesson that provides a philosophical overview to help you live an intuitive life.

An intuition exercise that demonstrates a technique you can use to integrate the lesson into your life.

An intuition journal that poses questions for you to write about. This will engage you in reflecting on deeper questions about the meaning of "creating the life you've always wanted" and what that life would look and feel like.

I know from personal experience and from working with thousands of clients that intuition is a ready source of direction—a compass of the soul—available to all of us, compliments of God, the Universe, Spirit, All-That-Is, or whatever we choose to call our personal understanding of Divine Intelligence. I don't want to impose my beliefs on you. I ask only that you be open to the vastness of the "Divine." To me, it means an invisible intelligence that animates our world and provides wisdom and love to guide our lives.

Fortunately, we all have the ability to tap into this power. We are all capable of developing it for practical use in everyday life, as well as for discovering and achieving life goals. I believe this wisdom comes to us through what we call intuition. Many people think of inner guidance as the domain of a gifted few, even though intuition is now recognized not as a rare, accidental talent but as a natural skill that most of us can cultivate.

Much of the wisdom I share in these pages is from the "school of hard knocks." I've had to learn these life lessons myself, and I continue to do so! I've also watched from a distance as my clients have struggled with them on their own journeys. There's no one, "right" way to use this book. You may want to use it as a week-by-week guide for the full fifty-two weeks of the year, read it cover to cover, or simply choose the chapters that resonate with you and focus on the intuition exercises and journal information in those sections.

Living an intuitive life is much more than simply paying attention to your intuition. It includes looking within for the answers, living life with courage, faith, patience, and trust. It also involves connecting with your Spirit through daily practice and taking action on the wisdom you receive. I believe the world would be a far better place to live in if we all knew how to routinely use the gift of intuition to create lives we love. My hope is that this book will assist you to connect with your "wisdom within" so you may live your life with enthusiasm, passion, and joy.

Compass of the Soul

LESSON 1

---◆◉◆---

Living an Intuitive Life

*The Divine consciousness speaks to our human
consciousness, offering us quick, keen insights
into the problems of everyday life and suggesting
potential solutions through the language of
intuition—the language of the soul.*

—Mona Lisa Schulz

What is intuition? Here are some of the more common answers.
Intuition is:

A tool for quick and ready insight.
A natural mental faculty.
A sixth sense we all possess.
A gut feeling.
A key element in the creative process.
A warning experienced as a tingle up the spine.
A component in problem solving and decision making.
A deep inner knowing.
A form of guidance and wisdom from God.

Intuition is a rich resource for acquiring knowledge about yourself and the world around you. It can offer guidance that allows you
to make the best choices for yourself. When you listen to intuition

and follow its wisdom, you will be led to a life that is full, success-ful, and rich with limitless possibilities. I believe that intuition is a connection to your soul, a vehicle for God (or the Universe if you prefer) to communicate with you. When you ask your intuition for help or insight, you are tapping into your Spirit and seeking its wise guidance. That's why I refer to it as "Divine Intuition."

Intuition comes in many forms. It communicates in different ways to each of us. Following are some of the ways intuition makes itself known.

Inner voice. Many people report a "still, quiet inner voice." Your intuition will always communicate with you in a compassionate, loving manner that is perceptibly different from your normal inner chatter.

Dreams. You can receive a wealth of guidance when you learn to ask for intuitive insight from your dreams.

Emotions. Intuitive information often comes through your feelings or emotions. You may simply "feel right" about a certain course of action. Or you might experience a sense of distrust about an individual or situation.

Physical sensations. The Japanese call intuition "stomach art." We call such sensations a "gut feeling." You might find that your body feels heavy if a decision you've made is wrong. Your body may feel light or experience "chills" if it is the correct path for you.

Instant knowing. You may receive a sudden flash of under-standing. This is sometimes called the "eureka" effect.

Symbols. Intuition often comes to us in symbolic images. It is said that "a picture is worth a thousand words." You might receive a symbolic impression of a rocky road if you choose Path A. If you choose the alternative Path B, you may see a clear, well-paved path in your mind's eye.

Coincidences and synchronicity. It's been said that coincidences are God's way of remaining anonymous. When you experience frequent synchronicity you'll know your intuition has led you on the right path.

While I have always wished that intuition would proclaim itself in a loud voice, saying, "Here's what you should do," it doesn't. Intuition has its own language, its own code. There is no one *right* way to hear its guidance. As you read this book, and as you write in your journal and try out the exercises, your own intuitive style will become clearer and more accessible to you. My hope for you as you proceed through this book is that you'll find a steadfast companion on your path in life, a true friend who wants what's best for you, who is always there, guiding, listening, encouraging—showing you the way to achieve your heart's desire through love and compassion. It resides within you and has been with you always. That companion is your intuitive guidance.

Intuition Exercise:
Create an Inner Sanctuary

To begin this exercise, think of a concern you have in your life right now. Perhaps it's a question about a relationship, a career choice, your health, or something about your spiritual development. Form this issue into a question that evokes more than a yes or no answer. Examples might be "What's the best choice for my career right now?" or "What steps could I take to improve my health?" or "How could I communicate more effectively with my boss?"

Choose a time when you won't be disturbed for half an hour. You may want to listen to a favorite piece of relaxing music. Sit quietly and close your eyes. Focus on your breath for a few moments. Slowly feel your breath coming in and then let it go out.

In your mind's eye picture a favorite place where you feel safe and comfortable. This might be by the ocean, under a tree in a beautiful meadow, by a babbling brook, or in a special room, either real or imagined. Use your imagination to make it even more attractive. See the colors becoming richer and deeper; listen to the sounds around you as you settle in; feel the emotions that this wondrous place evokes.

You are creating a sanctuary in your mind where you can go to receive intuitive guidance. Some people imagine their intuition coming to them in the form of a guide; others perceive the information in words, images, a felt sense, through body sensations or simply "knowing." Ask the question you formed at the beginning of the exercise. Wait. Take your time and use all your senses. What do you feel? What do you sense? What does your body tell you? What do you hear? What do you see? What do you know? Receive your answer in whatever form it comes. There is no right way, just your way.

When you feel ready, open your eyes and return to normal consciousness.

Your Intuition Journal

Each chapter of *Compass of the Soul* ends with questions to ask yourself. They're designed to help you get in touch with your own inner teacher—your intuition. Treat yourself to a beautiful notebook in which you can write your answers, or use your creativity and decorate a cover of a spiral-bound notebook with pictures and photographs that inspire you!

What did you learn from doing the exercise above?

What are the main concerns you have in your life right now?

Do you consider yourself to be an intuitive person?

What are the main ways that you receive intuitive guidance?

As you begin to deepen your understanding of intuition and pay attention to its wisdom, you'll be able to count on it as a reliable tool to help you create a life you love.

LESSON 2

———◉———

Happiness Begins Within You

*I am more and more convinced that our happiness or our
unhappiness depends far more on the way we meet the
events of life than on the nature of those events themselves.*

—Wilhelm von Humboldt

Part of learning to trust your intuition is to remember to ask,
"Does this decision make me happy?" or "Do I feel energized by
this decision?" There are many ways to ask the question and experience the answer, but here's the truth: your intuition will provide
you with information to make positive choices. Would it make
sense for you to be sent to earth with a magnificent inner guidance
system that made you feel awful? Not likely!

The root of the word *enthusiasm* is the Greek word *entheos*. It
literally means "God within." When you trust your *Divine* intuition you begin to feel better. You might even feel enthusiastic! We
often ask the wrong questions: "Why did this happen to me?"
"Why can't I make more money?" Your intuition works best when
you begin to put your focus on what you want, where you're
headed, and what your goals are. The question to ask is, "What
makes me feel lighter, more energized, happier?"

When I give people intuitive readings, I see their choices and
decisions as a form of energy. When you constantly put your focus

and attention on what you don't want or on what makes you un-happy, your energy stays stuck. You keep attracting the same old thing—relationships that don't work, lack of money, the wrong jobs—the same old issues time and time again.

It takes commitment to stay focused on what you really want. Here's the way I see it work in sessions with my clients. When they can get themselves thinking consistently about the new goal or objective through visualizing, affirming, and feeling excited about their intent, they begin to put out a new energy. It's as if they are putting forth a new signal to the Universe that says, "Here's what I want. Here's what I'm focused on right now."

I'm going to leave it to the quantum physics folks to help you understand how and why this process works. My intuition coach point of view is that it's as if the Universe reads the signal and wants to send you the perfect circumstance to match what you want.

Your inner guidance is always directing you to what makes you happy, healthy, and full of life. It will help you stay well or assist you in getting well if you're sick. It's the way your intuition helps keep you on track. When you consistently feel bad, it's as if the intuitive message is "Warning: You need to pay attention to what you're thinking and where you're headed." When you're feeling up, purposeful, and full of joy your intuition sends a different mes-sage. It says, " Stay on this path and continue. Good things are flowing your way."

Each and every one of us was born with an "intuition code." It's the wise part of you that knows your purpose in life and provides a constant outflow of information to assist you with the choices to live your purpose. Intuition doesn't require strain and effort. It is more a matter of relaxed and open receptivity. You shouldn't need to spend long hours deep in meditation to receive wise counsel. Just ask, then "listen" for the answer.

My client Angela has a difficult boss. She's often called in to meet with him on the spur of the moment. Before she enters his office she gets quiet, closes her eyes, and asks, "What do I need to know in order to have a beneficial meeting?" She focuses on her breathing, becoming very still. She gets into what she calls her "receiving mode" and allows the answer to take shape. Within moments an answer begins forming in her mind. It comes to her in images, words, and feelings. That's the way *her* intuition communicates with *her*. Get into the habit of checking in with *your* intuition throughout your day. Sometimes you may simply find that the answers pop fully formed into your mind. Other times, the answer may come when the pressure is off, later in the day. The more you practice, the easier the answers will come.

Intuition Exercise:
Envisioning the Perfect Outcome

The next time you're in a rut and want to get out of it, try this:

Ask yourself, "What would be the most perfect outcome to this situation?" Or, more simply, "What do I want?"

Write a paragraph or so about what you want. Don't try to figure out how you're going to get it. That's for your intuition to work out.

Close your eyes. Briefly bring to mind a situation that's causing your frustration.

Now bring to mind the outcome you want. Spend a few moments visualizing this perfect outcome. What feeling would you be experiencing if you got what you wanted? As you visualize this image, feel those emotions. Add some words to your imagery. Use whatever works for you. "This is great." "I feel terrific!" Imagine your friends and family celebrating with you. Do whatever you can to make this image real and vivid.

Ask your intuition, "Is there anything I could do right now that would make this happen?" Await a response.

Open your eyes when you feel ready.

Jot down any brief ideas, thoughts, or impressions you may have had.

Don't take action simply on what you *think* makes sense. Act only on impulses that *feel* like fun, make you excited, or seem enjoyable to you. Your intuition will begin to bring together the circumstances and synchronicities to create your goal.

Your Intuition Journal

Do what creativity coaches recommend: brainstorm. Begin to ask yourself the following questions. Write down any and all ideas; don't censor any of them.

"What do I want?" Or, simply, "What makes me happy?"

There are no right or wrong answers. Pay attention to any flashes of intuitive insight that come to mind regarding these new goals or wishes.

LESSON 3

Follow Your Bliss

I feel that if one follows what I call one's bliss—
the thing that really gets you deep in the gut and that
you feel is your life—doors will open up. They do!

—Joseph Campbell

What's your idea of a blissful life? Here's what I'd like to create in my life:

I arise early in the morning and go for a long walk in the woods or by the beach. I come back and have a healthy breakfast and go to my gorgeous, light-filled office that has a wonderful view of my garden. I spend a few hours at my computer working on my articles, books, and speeches. I return calls and plan a lunch date with a friend. I spend the afternoon talking to clients and discussing expansion plans with my business partner. I have time to make a leisurely meal for my family and to work in my garden after dinner. I look forward to traveling with my husband next week to a conference where I'm speaking about spirituality and intuition.

I am surrounded by close friends, family, and community. I'm healthy and my spiritual life feels strong and fulfilling. I enjoy creating dinner parties, and I have a wonderful home where I love to entertain friends. I have the abundance to own and decorate two homes. One of them is by the ocean on the west coast of Florida and another is nestled in the New England woods. I look forward to a trip to Provence in the south of France with my husband next month.

The game of life is about balance. It's about discovering what you love to do and serving others by doing it. It's about loving others and yourself. It's about doing work that suits you and rewards you. It's about caring for those around you—your coworkers, your kids, your parents and siblings, your friends, and people in your community. Living a life of bliss is about finding and being true to the inner voice that says, "This is what I was born for!" It's also having the courage to live that life joyfully and with passion.

Many of my clients are under the mistaken belief that when they follow their intuition all problems will disappear. Let me be clear. Part of being human is that we all have our ups and downs. It's normal to feel anxious before a big event and worried if you're laid off from a job. And you wouldn't be human if you weren't sad when a loved one dies. Our emotions are part of what we are here to learn from. They're part of our spirituality, and when we learn to embrace them we begin to heal.

Intuition will always guide you to a life of balance, peace, and understanding. When you honor it and trust its wisdom, your life becomes transformed. It points the way to a path you can follow that allows you to get from where you are to where you want to go. But how can you be sure that you're following your intuition to your ideal life, and not just responding to wishful thinking?

Easy. Accurate intuition makes you feel calm. It conveys information in a compassionate, loving, sure, and certain manner. When you are being guided to make a change in your life from the deepest part of your soul, you'll know it. I've asked people at my lectures how they know they're receiving a "yes" from the Universe. Here are some of the responses:

"My heart feels open."
"I feel safe."
"I experience a tingling, rushing energy up my spine."

"I just know."

"I receive spiritual images in my meditation—an eagle soaring, a moon glowing, or a picture of a serene lake."

"I feel like singing!"

"I feel full of joy."

"I feel like someone is giving me a hug or patting me on the back."

"I feel relief and a deep sense of letting go."

"I hear an inspiring piece of music. It's as if the heavens were singing."

As you move through these chapters contemplating your ideal life, remember these things and begin to discover the ways your own inner guidance gives you a thumbs-up sign. The art of listening to your inner guidance is invaluable. As you learn to tune in and ask for advice and direction, you'll be rewarded with an ever increasing sense of clarity and direction, allowing you to follow your heart's desire. It will never steer you wrong.

Intuition Exercise: Creating Your Ideal Life

One of the ways your intuition informs you is through your bliss! When you're happy about something, or you just enjoy thinking about it, that's your intuition giving you the message "Do more of this!"

What would a blissful life look or feel like to you?

Close your eyes and imagine yourself living this life. Put as much feeling and emotion into this image as you can. The ability to manifest your ideal life has a lot to do with your ability to feel a flow of clear, positive energy about what you want to create.

At present, don't try to figure out *how* you will create your ideal life. As you imagine, visualize, and feel it, trust that you are sending out an energy vibration to the Universe that will begin to attract what you desire.

Notice if there are any negative thoughts or feelings that arise as you imagine living a life you love. This, too, is helpful information from your intuition, and may indicate an area of resistance for you to examine.

Spend just a few moments every day doing this exercise and you'll find your heart's desire quickly attracted into your life.

Your Intuition Journal

All too often we focus on what we don't want, rather than what we do want. In your journal begin to expand on the answer to the question, "What is my ideal life?"

Do you feel it's possible to achieve this new life? If not, write a few sentences about why you don't think so. What's in your way?

Are you willing to try? What could you do to shift your thinking to allow for the possibility that you could have a life that's more enjoyable and fun?

If your intuition is saying "yes" to you, how do you know?

If your intuition is saying "no" to you, how do you know?

When you open to the possibility of a new life—one that feels open, enjoyable, and expansive—your intuition will begin to give you clues, hunches, and ideas to help you move in the right direction.

LESSON 4

—◦◉◦—

Become a Prosperity Magnet

I now draw from the abundance of the
spheres my immediate and endless supply.
All channels are free! All doors are open.

—Florence Scovel Shinn

Money (or the lack of it) is a highly charged issue for many people. I believe that money is neither spiritual nor nonspiritual, neither good nor bad. I've come to understand that money is simply energy that you can use in order to make your hopes and dreams a physical reality.

One of the observations I've made in my twenty-plus years of doing intuitive work is that we are made up of high-frequency vibrations. We are vibrational creatures. Every thought you think, every feeling you have sets up a specific vibrational pattern within and surrounding your body. Your emotions send out vibrational waves that appear to be magnetically charged. It's as if you are a walking magnet. You attract or draw to you what your emotions are broadcasting or vibrating. If you're constantly feeling bad about money, your love life, or your health, you focus on negative feelings that have a certain vibrational frequency, and thus will attract negative consequences.

People often feel hopeless about the prospect of creating more abundance. My client Mary stated the other day, "I've tried affirmations, visualizations, budgets, and investment classes. Nothing works. I'm still broke. I feel so discouraged." The energy vibration that goes out from Mary's set of thoughts and feelings is negative. Her car constantly breaks down, costing her a lot of money. Her investments don't produce the results she wants. She has been passed over for promotions (and raises) several times in the past year. She can't seem to save any money and constantly worries about her inability to plan for her retirement.

Conversely, when you're feeling good about yourself and your prospects for life, you magnetize positive things. Money begins to flow in, people are attracted to you, and synchronicities start to occur. Please understand that I'm not suggesting you simply put on a happy face, think positive, smile, and pretend everything is terrific when it's not. I'm talking about beginning to focus on the small things in your life that *do* work and that are evidence that you can attract abundance.

Intuition Exercise:
How Do You Feel About Money?

Think about the subject of money for a few moments. Allow yourself to imagine something you'd like to buy or a lifestyle you would have if you had more money.

Pause.

How do you feel when you think about it? Do you feel down and hopeless or does the idea excite you and make you feel energized and hopeful?

Your response is a valuable clue from your intuition regarding the beliefs you hold about money and your ability to magnetize what you desire. Did you have a negative or let-down feeling when you thought about money and all that it could create? What thoughts and beliefs do you hold about money that may have created that feeling?

Your Intuition Journal

Have you gotten into the habit of worrying about money, creating endless scenarios in your mind of being destitute and impoverished? It's time to reverse the cycle and use your imagination in a more positive and productive fashion!

What would you do if you were to unexpectedly receive one million dollars with the stipulation that you spend it on creating work you love?

What would you do if you were to receive so much that you could do whatever you chose to do for the rest of your life and not have to worry about money?

The answers to these questions are a strong message from your intuition about your life purpose. With the understanding that this money isn't in your life right now, what steps could you take to begin to live the life you dream?

Achieve True Abundance

*Please let me never forget how rich my life is right at
this moment. Please let me never forget that all I have
is all I need. Please let me never forget to give thanks.*

—Sarah Ban Breathnach

I have a client named Bill who is making close to $500,000 a year
and is constantly broke. He regularly talks about how there's never
enough. He fears he won't be able to get ahead. He's late paying
his bills. His checks to me often bounce, and he recently received
a foreclosure notice from his bank.

Joanne is a client who has a trust fund of several million dollars
and an annual income of about one million. I spoke with her on
the phone recently and she mentioned that she recently renovated
her home at the cost of $500,000 and bought a new Mercedes.
Plus, she had just returned from a monthlong stay in the south of
France. She expressed a great deal of fear about running out of
money. Hard to imagine, isn't it?

Last week I spoke with Kathy, who is a single mother of two
children. She started a small floral business several years ago. She
wanted to be self-employed so she could set her own hours to be
with her kids. She makes about $40,000 a year, regularly invests,
and has saved a small nest egg. She said, "I choose to focus on all

that I have. I see abundance all around me. I know that if there's something we need or want, we can find a way to make it happen."

As you look at these three profiles, who would you pick as the most prosperous? Perhaps the obvious answer is Joanne because she has the most money. Yet neither Joanne nor Bill *feels* prosperous. They constantly worry and fret that their money will run out. They spend profligately and have no confidence or faith in their ability to live a peaceful life with the money they have. Kathy, on the other hand, trusts her inner compass to point her in the direction of abundance, and she consistently experiences this in her life. She would be my choice for the most prosperous.

Here's my point. Your beliefs and ideas about money (or the lack of it) have the ability to attract or repel true abundance. Imagine that your thoughts are like magnets. What you focus on is drawn to you. It doesn't matter whether your anxiety about money is on the level of "Can I afford to pay for food this week?" or "Will I be able to pay for the new Mercedes I want?"

What is prosperity? Would you be prosperous if you had $500,000 in the bank? Would you consider someone affluent if she had $5 million? Is your neighbor who drives the Bentley fabulously rich? You may be surprised to learn that the vast majority of the world population considers *you* truly wealthy simply because you have a roof over your head, clothes on your back, and food on your table. So—why don't you feel prosperous?

The word *prosperity* stems from a Latin word that means to have hope, success, and good fortune. Prosperity is not a specific dollar amount. Prosperity encompasses many things. A colleague recently defined prosperity by saying, "I know that I have within me and around me a Divine flow of abundance. Whatever my goal, desire, or dream, I have the means and ability to create this thing or situation in my life."

Knowing how to create a prosperous life doesn't imply that everything you wish for will instantly be manifested. There is a duality of existence that is a bit tricky to master at first: 1) You feel thankful for all that you have. You see abundance around you and focus on it with an attitude of gratitude. 2) You also understand that you are constantly growing, learning, and mastering your world. It is natural for you to want more, to have fresh goals, and to move in new directions.

Intuition Exercise: Financial Gratitude

If you would like to attract more prosperity, try this experiment. Begin to focus on "financial gratitude." When you find yourself starting to feel anxious about money, or you catch yourself complaining about your lack of financial abundance, STOP. Now shift your attention to all that you already have. If you're very poor and have been focusing on your lack for quite some time, this may be a tough assignment. But it's important to begin.

Here are three recent items from my financial-gratitude journal:

- I feel blessed that my neighbor has a beautiful swimming pool I can use. I enjoyed a quiet half hour of relaxation after a day of writing. I don't have to own the pool or put money into the upkeep, but I reap many of the benefits.
- I enjoyed getting together with my friend Gail, who graciously paid for lunch. I value her friendship.
- I was about to place an order for audiotape duplication when a colleague sent me an e-mail about a service she uses. The new company provided the same service for about 30 percent less than the one I usually use.

When you find yourself feeling fearful and anxious, begin to consistently place your focus on all that you already have. This might be good friends, your health, terrific kids, an interesting job, or wonderful neighbors. Find anything to think about that makes you feel good. Gently shift your attention away from your fear and anxiety.

When you have quieted your mind, begin to shift your attention to what you want to create in your life. You'll find that as you consistently do this, your intuition will indicate the right thoughts, beliefs, and actions to attract what you desire.

Your Intuition Journal

In her book *Simple Abundance*, Sarah Ban Breathnach writes that a Gratitude Journal is a "polite, daily thank-you note to the Universe."
Here are a few questions for your *intuition* gratitude journal:

1. What do you want an abundance of in your life? (E.g., health, friends, prosperity, clients, love.)

2. Take a few minutes each day to write about how you received what you wanted. What are you grateful for?

As you begin to consistently take the focus off scarcity and place it on gratitude, you'll find your mood begin to lift. Opportunities will start to show up in your life where none seemed to exist before. Focusing on gratitude widens your channel of abundance and good fortune and allows good things to come to you more quickly.

LESSON 6

<hr>

The Power of Your Wise Self

*Patience is the front door to faith. If you come to
this door, know that you, your dream, and the Universe
are still moving into alignment but aren't quite there yet.
Be excited when you arrive at this point! This means
that you are doing your part as you should, and
your miracle is on the way to being born.*

—Sonia Choquette

Have you ever had a period of time in your life when *nothing* appears to be happening? No matter what action you take (or don't take) there seems to be no movement or change. Everything stays the same. I've observed that most of my clients dislike this time of transition, these pauses in life. It makes them feel uncomfortable. "I pray. I talk to my friends. I meditate. I read self-help books. I take action. I'm stuck. Nothing's happening!"

I have a different take on the matter. Often when I tune in to the person's soul and ask how I can be helpful, I hear, "Tell them much is going on in the unseen world. They are being prepared for the next step. Tell them to be patient, to wait, to have faith, and to find small joys in their present life. They will emerge from their hibernation soon."

I'm often given a symbolic picture that represents this transition state. I'm shown an image of planting bulbs in the cool ground of autumn and seeing them transformed into the beautiful blooms of spring. What I take from that image is that there is a Divine wisdom and timing for everything. In the fall and winter, those bulbs are being readied underground. They are unseen and yet they are experiencing the perfect conditions for their growth. Do they fret and thrash about exclaiming to all who will listen, "Nothing's happening! I must *do* something!" No. They wait and know that at the optimum time the earth will warm, the sun will shine at just the right brilliance, the rains will come, and they can fulfill their destiny to the joy and delight of all who see them.

Learn to cherish the lulls in your life. Spend time by yourself or with close friends. Read, take walks, appreciate nature, write in your journal, pray, meditate, nurture yourself, and listen to your wisdom within. You may not know what the next phase of your life will bring, but it will come. Be grateful for your rest. You are part of the flow of God's wisdom even if you appear to be standing still.

Intuition Exercise:
Ask Your Teacher

Have a pen, pad of paper, or your intuition journal ready for this exercise. You may want to play some of your favorite meditation music in the background. Close your eyes, take a few deep breaths, and say the word *relax*. Feel yourself slow down.

Pause.

Imagine you are floating upward into a beautiful, tranquil, and safe place out in the cosmos. You are going to this place to receive a higher wisdom. Many people just *feel* it rather than having a specific image of what this place looks like. Others report being in a cathedral or church or an illuminated garden. You may imagine it in any form that feels comfortable to you. This is a sacred place where you can go at any time, but especially when you feel stuck or are in a crisis. Profound love exists here. You are instantly wrapped in protection and caring beyond what you have ever experienced. See or feel the waves of light and energy all around you. There is wisdom and healing here in this place to assist you with anything you need.

Pause.

Imagine that you have a group of wise teachers who have come to provide guidance to you. See them surrounding you and sending you love. Talk to them and tell them about your concerns. They will converse with you and you will feel the answers pop into your mind. Say to yourself, "I am now opening to the information I need." Continue to have a dialogue for as long as the information you are receiving is helpful. Ask them what you are to learn through the transition you are experiencing. Ask if there is anything you are supposed to do. Ask them to help you with patience, faith, and strength during this time. Is there anything else they need to tell you?

When you feel complete, take some deep breaths, slowly return to normal consciousness, and write down the answers and impressions you received.

Many people worry that they are making up the answers. Others have questioned whether the information is from their intuition or a spirit guide or an angel. My response is that if the information is helpful to you and you feel better after receiving it, the source of the information isn't all that important.

Your Intuition Journal

Transitions happen to all of us. If you're goal-oriented, impatient, and driven these apparent lulls can be exceptionally difficult. It's hard to trust that the next chapter in your life will open. In order to gain some insight into your "transition style," see what your response is to the following questions.

What benefits are you gaining from a lull or transition in your life?

What do you like about this transition?

What don't you like?

What do you tell yourself about how you're supposed to be or act?

What can you do to comfort or nurture yourself through this phase?

Job change, illness, divorce, financial loss, and the death of a loved one are all at the top of anyone's list of major life stresses. If you're in the midst of one or more of these experiences, the turning point from crisis back to seeming normalcy often doesn't come as quickly as you might desire. The best question to ask yourself during times like these is, "How can I move through this phase in my life with self-care, love, and patience?" Pay attention to any answers your inner wisdom provides and act on the insight you receive.

LESSON 7

———◆◉◆———

Help Is at Hand

*Intuition is the subliminal sense that spirit endowed us
with to maneuver safely through the maze of real life.*

—Sarah Ban Breathnach

Have you ever gone through a terrible time in your life where one
bad thing after another befell you? You probably felt trapped and
feared that you couldn't find your way back to your "normal" life
if you tried. It's as if you found yourself deep in a forest and you
had no idea which path led you farther into the woods or which
path led you to safety. You may have wished during those times that
you had some kind of trail to follow that would bring you home.

Intuitive guidance can act like a beacon in your life and show
you the way to safety. It can lead you home to the peace, harmony,
and balance that is your birthright. But how do you tap into your
intuition when your mind is racing with fear and anxiety? Many
people report that when they're going through a major crisis they
have a hard time accessing their intuition. They feel that their guidance system has abandoned them. The stress you're experiencing just
calls for a different approach. Here are five ideas that really work:

Shift your perspective. This is not the time to think catastrophic thoughts about your future. Make a conscious attempt to

shift your focus away from any pessimistic thoughts. Use a short-term time frame for now. Try saying things to yourself like "I know I'll get through this." "What could I do today to make things easier?" "I am open and receptive to new ideas about how to improve my situation." "I've gotten through tough times before." "Something good will come of this."

Stay focused on the positive. During times of crisis it often feels like *everything* is going wrong, but that's seldom true. Staying constantly focused on what makes you feel bad will only worsen an already difficult situation. Pay attention to what *is* working. Perhaps a friend called to cheer you up, or your child got off to school this morning without a major tantrum, or you had a really nice lunch with a colleague. Find those precious slivers of appreciation in each day.

Be good to yourself. Most crises are self-limiting. That is, they don't last forever; they only *feel* that way when you're going through them. One way to make them a bit easier and open yourself to guidance in the process is to take some moments in each day and simply indulge yourself in something that makes you feel good. You might simply take five minutes to lie on the grass in your backyard, pet your cat, indulge in a tea break, or play some soul-stirring music on your stereo and kick up your heels.

Set short-term goals. Nothing restores your confidence faster than achieving a goal. Now is not the time to tackle big, long-term, difficult objectives. What are some small things you can do each day to make yourself feel better? Make a short list of manageable things you can accomplish that will help you reduce your stress. Here are five from a list I made during a recent stressful time: Order takeout at least once this week. Do stretching exercises for five minutes each day. Let my answering machine pick up my calls at night. See a funny movie this week. Get a massage. (And you thought goals had to be dreary!)

Intuition Exercise:
What Do You Appreciate?

It is often difficult for your intuitive guidance to flow to you when you're filled with fear and anxiety. It's almost as if the negative thoughts create a negative energy that surrounds you and rejects even the most valiant attempts of your inner wisdom to communicate.

Think about it: have you ever tried to provide emotional support to a friend who greeted your care and concern with a litany of negativity? Your friend might exclaim, "It will never get better. Nothing ever goes right for me. Things just get worse and worse. It's hopeless." Any wise words that you share with her when she's in that state are likely to fall on deaf ears.

If you find yourself sounding like this friend, read these next lines very carefully:

> Your circumstances are not causing you to feel bad.
>
> What you say to yourself about your circumstances is causing you to feel bad.
>
> Your bad feelings then contribute to and worsen the negative circumstances you experience.
>
> You need to stop feeding this cycle by beginning immediately to focus on what you appreciate in your circumstances right now or things will get even worse.

This is tough love, but here's a technique I want you to try if you are in a downward spiral of negativity. Each morning before you get out of bed I want you to choose one thing that you presently have in your life that you appreciate. This can be a very small thing or a very big thing. It can be as simple as the fact that you have a bed to sleep in, or that your dog likes you. It can be something bigger, like the fact that you still have a job or that you're reasonably healthy. It doesn't matter what you choose, just choose one thing each day.

Here's the exercise:

When you find yourself beginning to focus on what you don't want—for example, your lack of money, your ill heath, your concern about your child or your spouse—stop.

Begin immediately to focus on the thing you have chosen to appreciate for that day.

Keep the focus on the object of your appreciation until your mood starts to shift; then do something to distract yourself. In essence, you're trying to change the radio signal from WNEG to WPOS.

Your task is to get yourself into a place where you'll feel better. From that more positive place you can begin to feel more hopeful and can begin again to receive the messages from your intuition that you may have blocked out before. You are breaking a habit of thought and a habit of energy vibration that doesn't serve you. It's not unlike breaking any other habit. It requires patience and perseverance before it becomes automatic. If you will learn to do this technique diligently, your life will gradually change in a remarkably powerful way.

Your Intuition Journal

Have you ever found your thoughts careening out of control when you're in the midst of a crisis? You may find yourself imagining catastrophic happenings in your life or thinking up worst-case scenarios. At the very least it's difficult to find a peaceful place within when you're experiencing a life emergency. Here's a technique that might help: each morning write the answer to the following question in your journal.

What are you most grateful for in your life today?

Make it a mental habit. Whenever you find yourself feeling overwhelmed or upset, shift your focus to your "gratitude thought." That thought can act as an anchor when you begin to feel out of control. Instead of dwelling on an endless list of what is not working, dwell on what *is* working. Take deep breaths, slow down, and put your mind and imagination on gratitude. You'll be glad you did.

LESSON 8

—◈—

The Spiritual Journey

One can never consent to creep
when one feels an impulse to soar.

—Helen Keller

I am one of the world's worst meditators. However, every single book about spirituality that I've read insists on the importance of meditation. I find I get more anxious the longer I sit trying to quiet my thoughts and watch my breath, but I also understand the absolute value in doing it.

I believe that meditation connects you with the Divine. It allows the energy that is God to move through you, purifying you, releasing negativity, and energizing you. I believe that this energy also contains the wisdom of intuition, and tapping into it allows you to find new inspiration and direction on life's many paths.

Here are some ways to find peace with meditation. Give yourself permission to sit for just a short meditation. Many meditation teachers recommend a minimum of twenty minutes or more. However, I've found that beginning with the expectation of sitting for that amount of time can lead to failure. Instead, tell yourself, "I will meditate for five minutes." Have the intention of being still and being in the presence of God. More often than not, you may find that you remain meditating for fifteen or twenty minutes. You may feel like you're in a "no time" zone.

How do you "sit in the presence of God"? You just do. You sit. Quiet your mind as best you can and ask Divine wisdom to be present with you. It doesn't matter how you see or understand God. You may imagine a beautiful angel, a whisper in your ear, a feeling of exhilaration, or an inner knowing. Some people experience what they consider a messenger from God. They report feeling the presence of Jesus, Muhammad, Moses, Mary, or another spiritual teacher or more personal spirit guide. There is no *right* way to experience this. Your connection to Divine wisdom is for you alone.

Also try listening to music. It can help you focus. I have a portable CD player with a headset, and I play uplifting and angelic music. This serves to almost always put me in a more open, altered state.

I have always wished that God or my guides would appear with great fanfare and announce, "I am here. Here is the answer to all your questions!" However, I have found that true inner promptings are subtle. They come as nudges and whispers from my soul. That is why, despite my resistance, I find time to meditate. I find time to be still, go within, and listen.

Intuition Exercise:
Walk. Write. Dance!

Try experimenting with different forms of meditation to discover what works best for you.

Here are some options:

Try a walking meditation. This can be particularly helpful if you are really upset or agitated about something. Choose places where you can go for a quiet and undisturbed walk in the woods or other natural setting. Calm yourself by focusing on the present. Use all your senses, and observe and linger on all that is around you. Notice the fragrance in the air, the sounds of the birds, the breeze on your skin. Tune in to how you feel. As you become calmer, think about what has been disturbing your peace of mind. Frame it into a question, and as you continue your walk, listen for the answer.

Write in your journal. Writing is often a wonderful form of meditation. Don't try to have perfect spelling or faultless grammar. Your goal here is just to unwind with words. If you want to receive some guidance about a particular issue, try this. Take a solid block of time, say half an hour or so, and ask your intuition for answers. I find it helpful to simply write open-ended questions such as, "What should I do about _____?" Or "What is the best course of action regarding _____?" Don't attempt to censor your answers. Just write whatever you feel or whatever comes to mind. After your session or later in the day, go back and evaluate what you came up with.

Dance with intent! If you're an eternal fidgeter like me and find sitting meditation difficult, try the opposite: dance! My guidance has often indicated that it's a time in my life for a big leap of faith. Beginning a new book, speaking in a new venue, or appearing on a national television show are all examples of things that make me more than a little anxious. I have tried to sit, meditate, and visualize the perfect outcome to these situations, but I find it hard to focus. Instead, I put an uplifting piece of music on my boom box, close my eyes, and move. If you need courage, play "I Will Survive" by Gloria Gaynor. If you need a push to get going in new directions, put on "New Attitude" by Patti LaBelle. If you need to feel calm and go within for guidance, try one of Sanaya Roman's tapes (available at www.orindaben.com). Find some music that inspires you. I guarantee that you won't find this at most meditation retreats. But hey, it may work for you!

Your Intuition Journal

Write down questions you would like to ask your "spiritual adviser" (also known as your intuition!). Try this approach:

Make a statement about what you want and then ask an open-ended question. Following are some ideas to get you started:

"I'd like to make more money. What is the best way to do this?"

"I'd like to get along better with my sister. What's a good approach?"

"I want a career that is fun, profitable, and exciting. What are some options that would work for me?"

"I'd like to improve my ability to listen to my intuition. What steps should I take?"

Ask these questions as you try one of the meditations described above. You may find that the answers come more easily than if you were just doing a traditional meditation. Write the answers in your journal and take action on the information you receive. Take a look at your answers from time to time and see how the intuitive intelligence you received has shifted your thoughts in new directions. You'll probably be pleasantly surprised!

LESSON 9

———◉———

Embrace Love

*Our job as a teacher of God, should we choose to
accept it, is to constantly seek a greater capacity for love
and forgiveness within ourselves. We do this through a
"selective remembering," a conscious decision to remember
only loving thoughts and let go of any fearful ones.*

—Marianne Williamson

I had a funny experience today. I was driving on a narrow road
heading back to my house. An extremely slow driver was in front
of me. My mind was on the list of clients I needed to call back, the
e-mails that had to be returned, what I was going to make for dinner—you know how it goes. I was increasingly irritated with this
driver. I was imagining all sorts of bad things about him. He was
obviously being slow on purpose. He didn't care about the long
line of cars behind him. Who did he think he was, anyway?!

Finally, there was a break in the oncoming traffic and I sped up
to pass him. I turned to glare at this stupid man who was holding
up the traffic and was surprised to see my elderly next-door neighbor waving and smiling at me. I managed a sheepish grin and a slight
wave and made my way home about one whole minute before he
did, feeling very contrite.

I spent some time that afternoon thinking about the judgments I make about others. I don't like that I do it, and I realized it had become rather automatic. "She shouldn't dye her hair that color." "That guy's pants are too short." "I wish that neighbor would mow her lawn more often." When I begin to get into that critical frame of mind, I feel negative and depleted. Things irritate me all too easily. I know that when I feel that way I need to ask for guidance to enable me to shift my thinking.

I've begun an experiment. When I see someone about whom I'm ready to issue a negative judgement, I shift my focus. Now I ask, "What do I like or appreciate about this person?" The woman with the bad hair color had a wonderful outfit on, the guy with the short pants had a winning smile, and the neighbor who neglects her lawn makes brownies to die for.

When you continue to hold on to feelings of anger, hatred, and betrayal, you are the one who is hurt, not the other person. These strong negative feelings are indicators from your intuition that you need to come back into balance in some way. When you realize this, sit in prayer or meditation and ask for guidance that will lead you into a place of love and forgiveness. Inevitably, your thinking will begin to shift and you'll start to see the situation from a new and different perspective, one that feels more peaceful.

I truly believe that we are here on earth to have a reverence for life, to learn to appreciate, nurture, and love one another. Author and minister Mary Manin Morrissey writes, "Ultimately, what really matters is the love you give, the love you receive, and the love you leave. . . . We need to remember the three words to which it all boils down: Put love first." Intuition will always lead you to a loving place if you let it. There. Now I feel better!

Intuition Exercise:
Choose Peace

Think of a recent situation that made you feel irritated, upset, or judgmental. Write about it in your journal.

Sit quietly and allow yourself to connect with God. Simply feel a loving Presence fill and surround you.

Bring the situation you wrote about to mind. Ask your inner guidance to provide you with a more loving way to experience the situation.

You may feel a simple shift in perception or a sense of peace. Words may form in your mind indicating a new way of thinking about the situation. You may also find that nothing immediate happens but that over the next several hours or days, you receive helpful insight regarding the situation.

Your Intuition Journal

Feeling anger and rage about anyone or anything is a huge drain on your emotions and spirit. Recurrent thoughts such as "My parents did this to me" or "If only he would change, then I could be happy" place you in a victim position. You have a choice about your happiness. The amount of energy you waste thinking about the situation and the strong emotion you experience often cut you off from the loving communication of your inner wisdom when you need it the most.

Do you hold any resentment or grudges about a person or situation?

Describe the situation briefly in your journal.

Quickly answer the following question. Don't *think* about it too much. On a scale of 1 to 10, how much energy does this unresolved issue take?

Are you willing to choose to be at peace with this person or situation?

If yes, find a quiet place, tune in to your guidance, and write for several minutes answering the question, "How can I experience peace regarding this situation?" Don't edit what you're writing. Just write in brainstorm fashion. Put whatever comes into your heart and mind down on paper.

When you're finished, look back at what you wrote. What course of action will you follow? Write a one- or two-line synopsis.

The person who is harmed the most by anger or other strong emotions is not the person it's directed at; it's the person who is feeling it. If you recognized yourself in this exercise as someone who has a "victim habit," it's well worth the effort to break the chronic pattern of thought that is making you unhappy.

LESSON 10

—◆◇◆—

First, Know Yourself

*When I'm trusting and being myself as fully
as possible, everything in my life reflects this
by falling into place easily, often miraculously.*

—Shakti Gawain

Do you have a dream—some beautiful, idyllic life you would like
to live? For some of you, it may be to have scads of money to spend
freely. You could travel the world, eat in fine restaurants, and wear
the latest fashions. For others, it may be to live a simple life in the
country surrounded by a close-knit community of friends and family. Perhaps you've always admired someone who has your dream
job, or you imagine that you would enjoy their lifestyle. Your daydreams are messages from your soul. They inform you about your
life purpose and mission.

Since I was a child, I've had daydreams about speaking to an
auditorium full of people, writing books, and being interviewed on
television. This seemed like a ridiculous notion during my twen-
ties, when I had a series of low-paying jobs. My bottommost point
was a job in a department store, folding and organizing women's
lingerie after the frenzied activity of a sale. It was difficult to hold
fast to my dreams. I do remember thinking that at some time in
the future I would look back at that period in my life and laugh.

Many of you have given up on your dreams, seeing them as useless and impractical. Sometimes, if you've spent years denying the possibility of your wishes coming true, it's difficult to even say with certainty what those dreams might be. I'd like to give you permission to dream again. Pay attention when you catch yourself thinking, "I wish I could . . ." or "I hope that one day I'll . . ." Your daydreams may also come as images. When you have a few quiet moments to yourself, what do you find yourself fantasizing about?

All of this information is your intuition speaking to you! So many of my clients tell me their intuition has stopped communicating. It's true that if you ignore your inner guidance for long enough, its messages will appear to grow dim and fuzzy. It may almost seem to disappear.

Have you ever had a friend who was having a tough time? Maybe you listened with empathy and gave her lots of wise advice and counsel, and then she ignored you and did something that got her into even more trouble. You didn't want to give her more guidance until she was open to hearing it, did you? It's the same with intuition. It will remind you that it's there through your daydreams. Then it will wait until you're ready before it gives you more information about how to begin to make those dreams come true.

One client I spoke with several years ago struggled with the issue of how to live a simple life while still being a partner in the highly competitive law firm in which she worked. Her daydreams were full of images of sailing, being by the ocean, and living a life of peace. Instead of paying attention, she worked more and more hours to try to earn money. She was afraid she'd have to give up her lucrative and stimulating career in order to have the serenity she craved.

I spoke with her again recently. She had gotten sick and had had to take some time off. During the weeks of recovery, lying in bed, she'd begun to pay attention to her dreams again. She'd begun to ask the question, "How can I?" instead of "Why can't I?" At the end of her convalescence she'd transferred to another state—one by the ocean—and bought a houseboat. She lives on it year-round and describes it as an oasis of sanity in her rather fast-paced life as an attorney. She has created the best of all worlds.

Intuition Exercise:
The Power of Your Daydreams

Begin to pay attention to your daydreams. See them as information from your soul informing you of the direction to take in order to create greater peace and happiness in your life. Grab a cup of tea, close your eyes, and begin to remember the past and allow it to inform your future. Here are some ways to get you started.

Think back to when you were a child. Do you remember what you wanted to be when you grew up?

What were your favorite subjects in school?

Do you still have those interests today? If so, how could you begin to develop them in your present life?

What would you have considered a "fun day" when you were a kid? Perhaps it was being given a huge box of crayons and permission to draw all day, or gardening with your mom, or constructing a tall building with Legos.

What would you consider a "fun day" as an adult? (Who says only kids get to have a good time?!)

What were some career ideas that you eventually gave up? Are there any you might want to revisit?

If you had all the money you needed, what would you do during an ideal day, week, month, or year?

Think of five things you want to accomplish before you die.

When you look back at your list, what stands out? Were there any answers that surprised you? Which ones are you ready (and excited) about acting on? And here's the real question: Are you having fun yet?!

Your Intuition Journal

You may not even know that you daydream, but everyone does it! Begin to notice what you focus on when you drift into reverie, and jot some notes about what you're contemplating.

What do you daydream about?
What steps could you take to begin to make this happen?

Daydreams are an important clue about something that may be missing. What are you ready for in your life? Does your woolgathering take you to a beautiful island away from the demands of your work? Perhaps it's time for a brief (or prolonged) getaway. Do your thoughts drift to something more action-oriented such as mountain climbing, skydiving, or bungee jumping? You inner Spirit may be suggesting a little risk taking may be in order. When you begin to pay closer attention to your inner world, answers will appear. Trust those little nudges from your intuition, and opportunities will open up in your outer world.

LESSON 11

———— ◦◦◦ ————

Count Your Blessings

Until you make peace with who you are,
you'll never be content with what you have.

—Doris Mortman

We human beings are odd creatures. Have you ever noticed that when you finally reach a goal, you briefly congratulate yourself, sigh with satisfaction, and then immediately set about wanting something new and different? There's nothing inherently wrong with that. We seem to be hardwired to achieve goals, want more, and look to the future. The problem comes when you don't appreciate what you have, where you are, and what you've achieved. If you find that you're in a constant state of dissatisfaction with your life, you're not sending messages to the Universe that will attract a life of blessings.

You're probably familiar with the notion that happiness lies within. It's not guaranteed by a new job, more money, getting married (or divorced!), having children, or being able to retire. Any happiness, bliss, or peace that you experience is brought about by your attitude, thoughts, and beliefs. No new event or circumstance will secure your satisfaction; how you think and feel about the new circumstance will.

What do you feel grateful for right now? When you begin to focus on appreciation, your intuition will constantly provide you with information about how to create a life you love. It will give you nudges, hints, impulses, feelings, hunches, and dreams to move you in the right direction. In order to receive this Divine input, you need a channel that's open to accepting its messages.

If you're constantly stressed and always wishing for more time, money, freedom, energy—or something else—you need to create some time for what I call "sacred idleness." All those signs of stress are signals from your intuition that it's time to slow down or take a comfort break or give yourself a few hours or days off to reflect on your life. What do you truly want? What fills your soul? What can you let go of? What are the blessings in your life? These are all questions to ask your intuitive guidance system. Listen to the answers, reflect, and take action. Taking the time to meditate, write, and dream new dreams will pay off in a big way. They're the first steps in creating a life you love.

Intuition Exercise:
Journey to Peace

Do you have a favorite spot where you feel relaxed and at peace? It may be in your own home—in your favorite chair, sitting on the porch, or even in your bathtub. Perhaps it's outside your home. There is a waterfall a short drive from my house. I go there often with a picnic lunch and sit and watch the ducks and geese floating gently in the stream.

If you don't have your own special place, make it a goal to find one. Bring this book or your journal. What you need to do is very simple. Just be present. Observe what's around you. Take in your environment. Breathe. Relax. Just be with yourself and your surroundings. Slow down. If you find your mind wandering, notice it and simply bring it back to the present moment. Make time for sacred idleness. Feel your bliss.

Your Intuition Journal

Intuitive ideas and thoughts often come flooding in when we take the time to slow down. Make some time each week to sit quietly for a few moments. Ask yourself these two important questions:

> What are you grateful for?
> What can you do to have more quiet, spiritual time in your life?

The biggest complaint I hear is "I don't have time." Think about creative ways to carve a few moments out of your busy day. Perhaps you could take a short walk during a lunch break or get up fifteen minutes before the rest of your household and sit quietly in your favorite chair with a cup of coffee. You may find that if you simply take five-minute breaks for a breath of fresh air, you'll create a whole new lease on life.

LESSON 12

Your Body's Wisdom

Body symptoms become the language
that tells us we need to change something.

—Mona Lisa Schultz

For years I suffered with neck pain and accompanying migraines. I tried chiropractors, massage, yoga classes, acupuncture, analgesics, and a whole host of other things to reduce the sometimes disabling discomfort. Many of these techniques worked for a while or reduced the discomfort. However, I found myself wondering about the root of my pain. Why was it there? Was there a message it was conveying about my life? Was something out of balance? If I recognized it and did something about it, would the pain go away?

I went to a massage therapist after a day of particularly bad muscle spasms in my back and neck. I was lying on her table willing my body to relax under her expert hands. I heard this voice in my head repeating the words "I can handle this. I'm strong. I can make it. I'll just keep moving ahead and taking action." I realized that this was how I viewed myself and my life. I'm tough, strong, and independent and *I can make it!* There wasn't much room for vulnerability, dependence, or even a little bit of weakness or insecurity.

I want to emphasize that this was my own internal dialogue. No one was saying this to me but myself. Recognizing what I was saying made me understand that I was being extremely tough on myself and that I was *shouldering* a lot of responsibility because of this. That word was emphasized for a reason. I suddenly realized how metaphorical the body is. This shouldering of responsibility was causing me a great deal of physical and emotional pain in my neck, back, and shoulders.

I began to cry as the massage therapist continued to work on the knots in my muscles. I suddenly realized that I didn't have to be so strong and tough. I didn't have to hold myself to such high standards. It was okay to be vulnerable and ask for help, to admit that I didn't know something or even that I felt scared and uncertain about things in my life. I understood that I didn't have to be Superwoman with a long list of *shoulds* on her daily list.

I wish I could say that the neck pain went away at that very session. It didn't. It continued to diminish over time as I learned not to be so hard on myself and to reduce my expectation that I could do everything perfectly. Now, many years later, I only occasionally experience this pain. When it does recur I understand that my body is sending me an intuitive message. "Slow down. You are taking on too much and pretending you can do it all alone. Take time for yourself and get some support from your friends and family."

Intuition Exercise:
Healing Wisdom from Your Body

The body is an amazing messenger for intuitive information, and yet many of us ignore the important signals it provides. It could be a wise ally to provide valuable feedback about maintaining a healthy physical, spiritual, and emotional balance in your life. How well do you listen when your body gives you a "Something is wrong, please pay attention" message?

Here is an exercise to try when you find yourself with a physical symptom and want to receive intuitive information that could help your recovery. You may want to read the following into a tape recorder first, or have someone read it to you. Remember to go slowly. It's helpful to do this activity without judgment or criticism.

Take a full, deep breath and then exhale. (Pause.) Again, inhale deeply, all the way down into your belly, and then exhale fully. (Pause.) One more time—inhale deeply and exhale slowly. (Pause.) Begin to breathe normally again. Softly. Gently.

Allow your attention to drift to your physical body. Take whatever time you need. (Pause.) Begin to bring your awareness to a part of your body where there may be a physical problem, discomfort, anxiety, or distress. Let whatever wants to present itself emerge. (Pause.)

Where do you feel this issue in your body? (Pause.) Where does it reside? (Pause.) Take a moment to acknowledge the presence of this discomfort. (Pause.) Allow the possibility that your body may have a message for you about this physical concern. (Pause.)

Feel around the edges of the issue without being judgmental or critical. Let yourself experience this issue with all your senses. Does it have a color? (Pause.) A shape? (Pause.) You may even experience it as a taste or smell. What do you perceive? (Pause.) Is there an emotion associated with this issue? (Pause.) If it had a voice, what would it say? (Long pause.) The information you receive needn't make sense right now. You'll have time to evaluate it later.

Continue to experience this issue in any way that feels right to you. You might observe the issue from different angles or ask it questions. Remember to maintain a state of nonjudgment. Simply be curious about what you see, feel, hear, and experience. You are just exploring, staying open to any information that comes to you from your intuition. Allow the information to come. Don't force the answers. Whatever you receive is just information. (Long pause.)

Now, when you are ready, take a deep breath in and then slowly exhale. Know that you can come back to revisit this issue at any time. Inhale again and slowly exhale. Know that you may gather information after this exercise. Slowly come back to the room and open your eyes.

When you are fully back to normal consciousness, take your journal and write about your experience.

Begin to pay closer attention to your body. What messages does it send you? When you're tired, rest. When you're thirsty, drink. When you're hungry, eat. When you listen to and act on your body's signals, it will begin to reward you with good health.

Your Intuition Journal

Trying to understand the signals and messages your body gives you requires a little creative thinking at times. Some of these questions may seem a little odd, but be willing to try to answer them as they attempt to elicit the symbolic and metaphoric imagery often used by intuition to communicate its message.

What does your body feel like?

Where in your body do you experience tension, illness, or distress?

If you close your eyes and imagine this issue, what images come to mind?

If this issue were a shape, what would it be?

If it were a color, what would it be?

If this issue were an animal, what would it be?

If this issue were a symbol, what would it be?

If the issue had a voice and could communicate with you, what would it say?

If it had feelings, what would it feel?

Is there anything else that your body would like to say to you?

What can you do to resolve this issue?

What steps are you willing to take?

What did you learn from this exercise? Is there anything that surprised you? You might want to write the answers in your journal and come back to them a few days or weeks from now. Sometimes the answers become more obvious after you've had a chance to sit with them for a while.

LESSON 13

———◉———

Dancing with Life

A setback can lead us to a better place—if we'll just let it.

—Anne Wilson Schaef

There seems to be a notion out there that if you meditate, say your affirmations, think positively, and floss your teeth daily, no harm will befall you. Worse yet, there is a prevailing belief that if something bad happens to you, you have somehow *attracted* it—the idea being that you secretly wanted this awful thing to occur!

I have another theory. I think of setbacks, even seeming failures, as *redirectings*. Have you ever set out on a trip and gotten lost? I bet you've done what I have on several occasions—you stubbornly assumed that if you kept going in the direction you were headed, somehow magically you'd get there. As ridiculous as it sounds, it seems so much easier at the time than recognizing that you're wrong, stopping, checking the map, and turning around to go in the right direction.

Divine intuition works much the same way. It's as if a part of you, your soul, sees that you're headed in the wrong direction—away from your true purpose. This wiser self can see the overview of your life journey and wants you to be happy and on the right path. It will tap you on the shoulder a few times and give you some intuitive nudges, as if to say, "Hey, wake up! Wrong direction here!" If you continue to ignore those messages, eventually a crisis will begin to erupt.

I have a friend I'll call Bonnie who was a highly successful real estate broker. She was nationally recognized as a sales leader. She was on the go every day and night, including weekends. She believed that in order to retain her income and reputation she needed to give 150 percent to her career. Bonnie had no down time, no balance in her life, and after a while her health began to suffer. She discounted those intuitive nudges as merely symptoms of age and, ignoring them, continued at her breakneck pace. You can guess where this is going—she had a major health crisis and had to completely stop working. She was faced with a year of rehabilitation.

Over that year Bonnie recognized that her life had gotten dangerously out of balance. She began to meditate, write in her journal, dream, reflect, and create a new life for herself. She saw the seeming setback for what it was: a redirecting. Today she is healthy and in a successful new career as a coach helping others with life direction and balance.

Intuition Exercise: Feeling Good Again

Sit quietly. Close your eyes and take a few deep, relaxing breaths.

Think of a time when you felt joyful, relaxed, and at peace in your life. Spend a few moments savoring those memories. Remember the people you were with, the activities you were involved with, the home you lived in. Do whatever it takes to make the scene and your feelings as vivid as possible.

Ask your intuition this question: "What could I do to bring these good feelings into my life again?"

Pay attention to any thoughts, feelings, impressions, and body sensations you have. Your intuition communicates with you in many ways. You may find that the answer doesn't come to you immediately. That's fine. It may come in a dream. Or later in the day, you might just "know" the answer.

When you feel ready, open your eyes and return to normal consciousness.

Your Intuition Journal

If you think of a pie chart, what percentage of your time and energy do you currently allocate to work, social life, spiritual life, family, fun, or any other area that is important to you? Do you feel as if some part of your life is currently out of balance? If so, here are some questions for you to consider for your journal.

What could you do to bring good feelings and balance into your life again?

What steps are you willing to take to bring back more balance?

Expect a few setbacks; they're a natural part of the process in creating a life you love. Don't view them or yourself as a failure because you ran into an obstacle. Pick yourself up, continue to experiment, and proceed with all the fearlessness you can muster. Ask yourself what you learned and get back on your path. Take some small steps toward your dream, and keep walking!

LESSON 14

—◦◉◦—

Live Your Life with Joy and Passion

*Illumined spiritual teachers die of heart disease and
cancer just like the rest of us, while cantankerous
pessimists who smoke cigarettes and eat lots of
hamburgers sometimes live to be a hundred. And all
of us, no matter how many bean sprouts we eat, miles
we run, affirmations we say, hours we meditate, and
how hard we pray, are all going to die sometime. The
question is not whether we will die, but how we will live.*

—Joan Borysenko

How do you live your life? As the above quote from Borysenko seems
to say, we can torture ourselves doing all the *right* things in order
to guarantee—what? That we'll go to heaven, live the longest,
win the "Most Spiritual" award, make the most money, or have the
most toys when we die? So often we suffer and tolerate less-than-
ideal circumstances because we believe that there is a reward, a
payoff for all this good behavior somewhere in the future.

What about now? Researchers have shown that people who are
the happiest are the ones who simply expect that things will work
out well, who take pleasure in the simple events of their lives, who
expect others to like them, and who try to the best of their abilities to see the good in people. They understand that life will have

its ups and downs, but they try to maintain their focus on the good.

While we're not all hardwired to be optimists, we do, however, have tremendous power by way of our own thoughts and attitudes to live a healthy and happy life. When you're feeling down or worried, practice shifting your focus to anything in your life that you are grateful for. Do it anywhere—while you're sitting in the middle of traffic, making a meal, getting ready for bed at night, or waiting in line. If you can make "right now" a pleasant moment, free of stress, you can string together many of those moments into a day, a week, a month. Who knows—your future may take care of itself!

Following your intuition and shifting your focus to gratitude won't guarantee a life without heartache and hardships. It will, however, lead you to the surest path for creating peace of mind and tranquillity of spirit whatever your circumstances.

Intuition Exercise: Living the Good Life

Here's a quiz. Put a check next to all the following that are true for you. Be honest, now; no one else has to see this but you.

_____ I feel overwhelmed on a daily basis.
_____ I take care of everyone's needs but my own.
_____ I feel depressed.
_____ I don't sleep well.
_____ I'm constantly tired and cranky.
_____ I look forward to each day with enthusiasm.
_____ I take time to do fun and rewarding things.
_____ I feel enthusiastic.
_____ I wake up feeling rested.
_____ I feel energized as I go about my day.

There is no big secret to this little quiz. I'm not even going to ask you to score yourself. I'll just invite you to observe how many of your check marks were in the first five statements and how many were in the second five. The answers are obvious. The question to your intuition becomes, "How can I live my life in such a way as to be filled with enthusiasm?" The answer to that question may be in letting go of something that drains you and replacing it with something that begins to excite and entice you.

Your Intuition Journal

In order to create a life you love, you'll need some information about what that could look and feel like. Here are the questions for your journal:

What brings you joy?
What do you feel most proud of?
How will you know when you're successful?
What steps are you willing to take to bring more joy into your life?

Everyone is going to have a different definition of success. For some it will be the amount of money they have or the kind of house they own. Others will feel successful because they've raised a wonderful family or overcome adversity. Only you have the right answer for you.

LESSON 15

Divinely Guided Steps to Change

On the ladder of success some people are at the top of the ladder, some are in the middle, still more are at the bottom, and a whole lot more don't even know there is a ladder.

—Robert Schuller

I am an impatient person. I don't like that I am, and I try to work on this aspect of myself constantly. I remind myself to slow down, to enjoy my life in the moment, and to experience gratefulness for all that I have. I have to confess that this doesn't always succeed. For example, *Divine Intuition* had been in the bookstores for only two weeks when I jokingly asked my assistant, "Why isn't it a best-seller yet?!" (I was only half kidding.)

I know I'm not alone in this experience of restlessness. I hear it from my clients all the time. "I've tried affirmations, visualizations, and listening to my intuition. It doesn't work! Why don't I have what I want yet?" You may wonder if you're doing something wrong, saying your affirmations improperly, or misidentifying your intuition and making bad choices. I've discovered that life doesn't seem to go in a straight line for most of us. Despite what many self-help books imply, you don't usually sail effortlessly from the completion of one successful achievement into another.

The Universe is at work behind the scenes helping you climb the ladder to your success. There is a Divine intelligence that knows exactly what you need in order to grow into the next, new experience you want to create. Susan Jeffers writes in her wonderful book *End the Struggle and Dance with Life,* "When we are spiritually evolving, we are in a better place to handle whatever life hands us." She adds, "We all want quick and easy, but when it comes to becoming a spiritual being, speed doesn't work."

I've had many experiences in my life that felt like failures. At the time it was hard to imagine that I was anywhere near to achieving the goals I so desperately wanted. Yet when I look back at those situations with a few decades of hindsight, I can see that the Universe had put those seeming detours in my path to help me grow into my vision.

While it may have appeared to me that nothing was happening, the changes that were taking place in my emotions, thoughts, and spiritual growth were profound. It's as if Divine intelligence knew exactly what I needed to overcome the limiting beliefs I held about myself and the world. God was readying me for what I needed in order to be able to achieve the next steps in my life.

You may think your goal is to get that promotion, to find your life partner, or to write a best-selling book. There's nothing wrong with that! However, God uses your desires to help you learn about love, forgiveness, kindness, community, wisdom, and patience along the way. Trust and faith are the qualities to focus on while the forces of universal wisdom do their work to assist in your spiritual unfolding.

Intuition Exercise:
Powerful Questions for Change

Life presents us with a series of ups and downs. There may be areas of your life that are going very well and other parts where you feel stuck and anxious about what to do next.

Close your eyes, take several slow, deep breaths, and imagine that you have a very wise, spiritual teacher sitting across from you.

As you breathe in, feel the profound love, acceptance, and compassion that your guide is sending you. You feel filled and surrounded by these qualities. Sit with this experience for a few moments.

There are three questions for you to ask your teacher. Pause after each and listen for the answer.

"What am I learning right now?"
"What can I do to find peace in my present situation?"
"Is there anything I need to do?"

Open your eyes and write down the answers you received.

It's a common experience to feel as if you are "making this up." You may receive the answer in a feeling, words may pop into your mind, or you might simply just know the answer. These are all ways that inner guidance speaks to you. If the answers you perceived make you feel calmer and less anxious, trust that what you received was your Divine Intuition.

Your Intuition Journal

If you're currently struggling through a challenging time in your life, it might help to think about a period when you experienced something similar. Most crises tend to be self-limiting. (Although it often doesn't seem like that when you're going through one!) Here are some questions to consider for your journal.

What are three of the most difficult situations you've faced in your life?

What qualities did you develop as the result of those difficulties?

In what way did those difficulties prepare you for goals you later achieved?

What insight did you discover in considering these questions? You might find it helpful to say to yourself during difficult times, "I've gotten through times like this before. I'm strong [or resourceful, courageous, intelligent—whatever word fits for you]. I'll use this quality to help me get through this, and things will work out. I just need to be patient."

LESSON 16

—◉—

The Life You Were Born to Live

*Here is the test to find whether your mission
on earth is finished: If you're alive, it isn't.*

—Richard Bach

Try a simple experiment. Find a comfortable place to lie down for
ten minutes or so and daydream about what an ideal life would
look like to you. See yourself achieving your goals, imagine yourself doing all the things you most enjoy. Don't read any further
until you've done this.

Okay. Did you do it?

In doing this exercise with my clients, I've found that people
divide themselves loosely into two categories. The first group
emerges from this brief daydream fantasy with excitement in their
voice. They can tell me in detail what their ideal life looks and
feels like. They're on their way to success. The second group will
begin by informing me about all the issues that will stand in their
way—not enough money, an inadequate education, an unsup-
portive spouse, low self-esteem. You get the picture. They usually
talk themselves out of their dream before they begin.

The dreams, fantasies, and goals that fill your consciousness on
a daily basis are part of the way your intuition speaks to you. What
excites you and makes you feel passionate is what you were born

to do. Those feelings are *life energy* flowing through you. When you feel enthusiasm for something, ask yourself how you can move *with* this energy rather than away from it.

In the book *Harry Potter and the Chamber of Secrets,* the great wizard Dumbledore says to Harry Potter, "It's our choices, Harry, that show what we truly are, far more than our abilities." You have a choice to believe that you have it in you to create success, or that you have too many obstacles in your path. Which do you choose?

Intuition Exercise: Slow Down and Listen

Many of us have lives that are so busy, it's hard to hear our "still, small inner voice," much less have the time to act on its wisdom. For this intuition exercise, your assignment is to *slow down*. What does this mean in reality?

> Leave early for an appointment so that you have time for a walk and some fresh air before your meeting.
>
> If you're one of those people who always stays late at the office, leave on time.
>
> Make yourself a nice meal or call a friend to join you at a restaurant.
>
> Take a slow leisurely walk through your neighborhood or around where you work. Practice being aware of all that is around you.
>
> Make an appointment in your calendar for a free day, where you have nothing planned.
>
> Remind yourself to simply *stop* and take some slow, deep breaths for a few moments several times a day.

What are some things you enjoy doing that make you slow down and appreciate life? Do *at least* one of these every week.

What does all this have to do with intuition? When you allow some quiet, peaceful time into your life on a daily basis, you give that still, small voice of Spirit a place to slip in and grace you with its wisdom. An all-pervading force of love and wisdom fills you and surrounds you. It wants you to be fulfilled and happy and to live the life you were born to live.

Your Intuition Journal

Think back to three times in your life when you felt fully engaged and excited about something you were doing. What memories come to mind? Write about these in your journal. Here are some questions to prompt further insight.

What common theme runs through these three experiences?

What can you do now that would bring some of that excitement and enthusiasm back into your life?

Remember that you don't have to make a big change. Begin with something small. Often when you take one small step after another, you begin to see options that hadn't seemed to exist before. Be willing to move toward what you're enthusiastic about, and your life will begin to change in miraculous ways.

LESSON 17

——◆——

A Simple Plan for Your Success

*A successful day: to learn something new; to laugh
at least 10 times; to lift someone up; to make progress
on a worthy goal; to practice peace and patience;
to do something nice for yourself and another; to
appreciate and be grateful for all your blessings.*

—Michael Angier

I'm a true fan of self-help books. I grab them off the bookstore
shelves and read them as soon as they come out. I keep a stack of
five or six of them by my bed and read them before going to sleep
at night. I think some of them are filled with ideas that are far too
complex to fit into your daily life—unless you have nothing else
to do! Following is my distillation of some of these ideas, but with
an intuitive spin on them.

What do you love to do? Successful people pay attention to
what they feel passionate about. They commit to spending time
each day doing what they love. For some it's a job that pays. For
others it may be volunteer work or simply a hobby. Begin to notice
when you feel excited about something. That's a clue about what
to pursue.

Practice gratitude. Ample evidence exists that you get what you focus on. Do you often whine and complain about what you *don't* have and ignore the abundance all around you? Begin to notice and appreciate what you attract easily into your life. Perhaps you have a healthy body, or a wonderful group of close friends. Notice small things around you—the new flower that has emerged in your garden, the sound of your cat's purr, the laughter of a child, or the beauty of freshly fallen snow. Before you know it, abundance in all forms will begin to flow into your life.

Trust your inner wisdom. People who believe in trusting their intuition tend to be more successful in life. It doesn't appear to matter how they receive this information, whether it's through a wise angel, a spirit guide, or just an old-fashioned "gut feeling." Learn to pay attention to how you receive these impressions for yourself and check in often with your inner "intuitive success coach."

Acknowledge your achievements. How often have you worked really hard to attain a goal and then never given yourself credit for your achievements? I keep a running list of things I've accomplished each day, each month, and each year. If you do this you'll probably discover you've created more successes in your life than you had previously imagined. Success builds on itself.

Practice positive self-talk. I can't stress this one enough. What you say to yourself on a regular basis becomes what you experience in your life. Become aware of the inner dialogue you have with yourself. Request guidance if you need help with this. One client asked in prayer, "Please guide my thoughts, my words, and my actions. I wish to think, speak, and act with love." She was astonished at the difference this simple affirmation made.

Choose to be happy. Research has shown that happiness is a choice. It is not necessarily dependent on life circumstances. There is always a positive *and* a negative aspect to any change that occurs in your life, but it's your choice to select your focus. Get in the habit of asking, "What's good about this situation?" When you continually select that way of viewing the world, you will discover that happiness finds you!

Intuition Exercise:
Trusting the Process

Your intuition is present in your life to help you create a life you love. When you take the time to check in, listen, and act on the guidance you receive you will always be led in the right direction. Begin to acknowledge the presence of this wise counsel. See which one of the following statements or questions work for you whenever you need intuitive information.

"I know what's best for me."
"Things are falling into place."
"What do I need right now?"
"Everything is working out."
"The wisdom I need will come to me as I need it."
"What outcome feels best right now?"
"What is the best outcome in this situation?"
"What is the most loving (or Spirit-filled, forgiving, wise) decision right now?"
Your job is to:
Ask.
Trust.
Receive the answer through thoughts, images, feelings, words, and knowings.
Act on the wisdom you receive.

Your Intuition Journal

Deciding what your proudest moments are is a great way to identify your core life values. It helps you define both where you are now as well as what you want to head toward in the future.

What are you most proud of accomplishing . . .

today?
this week?
this month?
this year?
in your life?

Having completed the above list, what new insights do you have? Is there a theme you can identify? As you look over your list of accomplishments, you may discover that the challenges you experienced provided you with an opportunity for profound growth, insight, and positive change.

LESSON 18

—◆◉◆—

The Power of Intention

*When you are inspired by some great purpose, some
extraordinary project, all your thoughts break their
bonds; your mind transcends limitation, your consciousness
expands in every direction, and you find yourself in a new,
great and wonderful world. Dormant forces, faculties
and talents become alive and you discover yourself to
be a greater person by far than you ever dreamed.*

—Patanjali

Something almost magical begins to occur when you make a major
decision. A powerful energy is released from you into the Universe.
You bring together your belief in yourself, your goals, your intui-
tions, your hopes, and your dreams into one big cosmic intention.
It's as if you've said to the Universe, "This is what I want in my
life. Help me make it happen!"

Your clear goal or intention sets off a chain reaction. There is a
German proverb that says, "Begin to weave and God will give you
the thread." When you decide and begin to take action—even a
small step—the Universe is on your side, conspiring with you to
bring about your dreams.

When you can stay in a place of focus and clarity regarding your
goals, you'll find evidence that your intentions begin to manifest

COMPASS OF THE SOUL

quite quickly. However, if you're like most people, you may find yourself getting sidetracked by feelings of confusion, impatience, and fear. Doubt sets in, and your once lofty aims seem to recede into the background.

How can intuition help you navigate the minefield of conflict you may experience between the birth of an intention and the manifestation of the results in your life? There are three main roadblocks that I see people running into: 1) You can't logically figure out how you can get from where you are to where you want to be. 2) Doubt and fear set in and you begin to question whether your goal was right to begin with. 3) You get caught in the nether-world between being too passive in achieving your goal and too active.

You *can* get there from here.

The Universe has a remarkable way of helping you achieve whatever your thoughts and intentions are focused upon. Think of it as an invisible source of power, wisdom, and knowledge that is readily available to help you create your heart's desire.

My friend Jeannie told me a charming story about how she met her husband. It perfectly illustrates how this invisible power can create miracles. She had ended a relationship with a boyfriend who had not wanted to make a commitment. Jeannie had really wanted to get married and begin a family. She had joined dating services and answered personal ads, all to no avail. She'd told me that in desperation she'd prayed about it and put it in God's hands.

A few days later she went to a community fair with some girl-friends. They were walking down a path from their cars to the fair when they noticed two men behind them. Just at that moment an old man leapt out of the bushes, pointed at Jeannie and at one of the men, and said, "You two should talk to each other!"

Jeannie said they were all startled, but then they joked for a few moments and exchanged pleasantries. When she looked back to acknowledge the old man, he was, oddly, nowhere in sight. The group continued their walk to the fairgrounds and had a great time together. Larry asked Jeannie to join him for dinner the next day, and the rest, as they say, is history!

Can you remember a time or times in your life when you attained something through seemingly miraculous means? The Universe has infinite means at its disposal to help you reach your goals. Your job is to pay attention to all those things that make you feel alive, happy, and joyful, and to keep yourself in that "feeling good" space. Then let God handle the details.

It's normal to feel a little anxious and to experience doubt whenever you make a change in your life. Making a decision to alter the status quo takes you out of your comfort zone. If you're finding that the discomfort is keeping you stuck, it's helpful to ask your intuition for some guidance. When you have an overabundance of fear, there is usually a significant limiting belief or internal conflict that prevents you from moving on to the next step in your growth.

Any strong emotion is a piece of information from your intuition. It can provide a valuable clue about what might be holding you back. Ask your intuition, "What am I feeling anxious (or fearful, worried, or upset) about?" For example, imagine that your goal involves a career change where you could conceivably make a lot more money. If you had a core belief that making money wasn't spiritual or that for some reason you weren't worthy of achieving this promotion, you would experience a significant inner discord. You can easily see how these limiting beliefs might cause you to feel uncertain and anxious.

See if you can pinpoint the beliefs, values, and thoughts that are at the root of your uneasiness. "What new belief will allow me to resolve this conflict and to feel confident?" Your intuition may have been directing you to create this new goal for the very purpose of helping you let go of your limiting belief. Resolving it will free up a huge amount of energy and allow you to more easily create a life you love. Your intention in asking this question is to find an answer that makes you feel open, certain, and clear.

Intuition Exercise:
Small Steps to Success

It's all too common to fear that you've made the wrong decision and to attempt to go back to what you've known. Let's face it: no one likes to get out of their comfort zone without a guarantee of success. Here are some questions to put your intentions to the intuitive test:

Does your goal make you feel alive, happy, and enthusiastic?

Are you willing to devote some time and energy to it each day this week and in the weeks to come?

What is your strategy to deal with the inevitable fear and discouragement that will occasionally come along?

Have you created time for meditating, dreaming, visualizing, and affirming your goal?

Are you continuing to ask your intuition for guidance by posing questions like "How can I create this goal?" or "What are the next steps I need to take in order to create this goal?"

Have you let go of things that drain you and made space in your life in order for your goal to expand and grow?

Your Intuition Journal

Write about an occasion where you have achieved a goal through a series of coincidences and synchronicities. To jog your memory, think about how you met your spouse, landed a job, or found the perfect apartment. Perhaps there was an occasion when you needed money for something and it arrived in an unexpected way.

When you can bring to mind all of the amazing miracles that have occurred, it will help you have the faith you need whenever your life takes an unexpected turn.

LESSON 19

—◈—

The Magic of the Present Moment

*It's only when we truly know and understand that we have
a limited time on earth—and we have no way of knowing
when our time is up—that we will begin to live each
day to the fullest, as if it were the only one we had.*

—Elisabeth Kübler-Ross

Is something missing from your life? Do you often feel empty or dissatisfied? I recently met with a client I'll call Mary Ellen. She described feeling somewhat depressed and anxious a great deal of the time. She said, "I want something more in life, but I can't imagine what it is. It's as if part of me is missing."

As she continued to talk, it became clear to me that Mary Ellen was doing things for everyone in her life except herself. She took care of her niece after school, worked a full-time job as a book-keeper, helped care for an ill family member, and was a single mother for her nine-year-old son. I asked Mary Ellen if there was anything she did on a regular basis that was just for her. She looked at me blankly and said, "I don't have time."

Does this sound like you? Here's a simple truth: in order to create a life you love, you must first make room for it in your life. When your life is filled up with too many people, situations, and things that drain you, there's no space for something wonderful and new.

As I talked to Mary Ellen she casually mentioned that she liked to paint but hadn't picked up a paintbrush in years. I pointed out to her that when she spoke about her artistic interests she lit up and became energized. "This is your intuition giving you a step you can take in order to bring some passion and excitement back into your life," I said. I suggested that she might want to take an art class at a local adult education center. She agreed.

For the rest of our session we discussed how to create some free time so she could take this class. By the end of the hour, we had decided that she'd talk to both her sister and her ex-husband about sharing more child-care responsibilities. She sent me an e-mail a couple of months later, telling me that she had freed up two evenings a week and had enrolled in a painting class.

What does creating space in your life have to do with intuition? You may be doing all the exercises I mention in this book—writing in your journal, meditating, affirming, visualizing—and still not be getting the results you want. Your intuition may be providing you with great ideas for change and working hard at bringing opportunities your way. What does your intuition encounter when it has done its job? "Go away. I'm too busy! I don't have time for change right now." Take time to listen to these ideas and see what unfolds.

Intuition Exercise
What Excites You?

As I stated to Mary Ellen, one of the ways intuition communicates with you is through what you feel excited about. That's an important piece of input you should pay attention to, because it's providing you with information about a step that you could take. Begin to make time for it in your life.

1. *What did you once feel excited about?* You may want to think back to when you were a kid. Was there something you particularly enjoyed as a child that you haven't done

in years? That may give you a clue about what to write about. Collect these in your journal.

2. *What drains you?* Here's a question to ask yourself when you're considering what to let go of: "Is there a person or situation that makes me tired and irritated just thinking about it?" That's another clue from your intuition.

3. *What steps could you take to change the above situation?* Identifying what drains you does not give you permission to immediately get divorced, quit your job, or disown your family! You may need to set better boundaries with someone or have an honest conversation. Explore new job opportunities or simply begin to confront your desire to please everyone in your life and begin to say "no" more frequently.

4. *What are you willing to do to create space?* Simply understanding that you need space isn't enough. You'll need to create a plan of action. What are three steps you could take to free up some time for yourself? Write them in your journal.

5. *What steps are you willing to take to bring fun, excitement, and passion back into your life?* This does not need to be something huge. We're talking steps, not flying leaps of faith! You could make a lunch date with a friend, enroll in a class, take a walk in the woods, play with your kids, romp with your dog, or dig in your garden. None of these will make a profound change in your life. But it's a beginning. It's saying to the Universe, "I deserve to take time for me. I am worthy of receiving wise intuitive guidance. I now have room in my life to cherish the message and act on its wisdom." When you do that consistently—watch out, life! Here you come!

Your Intuition Journal

Do you frequently complain about a person or situation? Is there something or someone high on your list of frustrations? If your immediate response is "yes," that thing or that person probably takes a lot of your energy.

In your journal list five things that are currently draining your energy.

You have three options regarding each item on the above list: 1) you can keep the status quo; 2) you can change one or all of them in some way; or 3) you can let them go completely. What are you willing to do?

LESSON 20

——◦◉◦——

Your Heart's Desire

*Desire directs focus. If your desires are vague, your focus
will be blurred. If your desires are heartfelt, however, your
focus will be sharp and clear. . . . Clear focus is the mind's
magic wand. . . . Wherever you clearly focus, you create.*

—Sonia Choquette

If you could follow your heart about one thing right now, what
would it be? The answer to that question is part of your inner guidance system. Your heart knows what your head (or your intellect)
often doesn't. Your heart is like a divining rod able to receive and
translate messages from God.

Has there been a longing in your life for more time, balance,
love, or freedom? Perhaps you're in a rut and desperately want to
take a risk and break out. You may admit that you're hungering for
more in your life, but you may not trust your instincts, or you try
to repress or deny your heart's wisdom. Take that first step to recognize and validate that you want something more. Recognize the
guidance from your intuition alerting you that it's time to move in
a new direction.

You may simply be aware that your heart's emotions are signaling that it's time for something new, but you don't know what to
do. Remember, this needn't be a big, bold step. You might be

inspired by starting with a small change in your routine or a willingness to try something new. Perhaps it's as simple as leaving work a little earlier one night this week, or going for a walk before breakfast some morning. You are simply letting the Universe know that you want to set the energy in motion to create the shift that you want to occur. Be willing to try something new and begin the path to your heart's desire.

Intuition Exercise: Energizing Your Life

Close your eyes and think about various aspects of your life. In your mind's eye, go over a typical week. As you do, notice where you feel uplifted and excited and also where you feel down or enervated. Those are important intuitive messages. Spend about five minutes on this part of the exercise.

Now look at the following statements. What's working in your life? What's not working? On a scale of 1 to 10, ask yourself how content you are in these areas. Circle the number that feels closest to your answer. The last two items allow you to create statements of your own.

I enjoy my work.	1 2 3 4 5 6 7 8 9 10
I take time for myself.	1 2 3 4 5 6 7 8 9 10
I feel intellectually challenged.	1 2 3 4 5 6 7 8 9 10
I eat a well-balanced diet.	1 2 3 4 5 6 7 8 9 10
I have a community of friends.	1 2 3 4 5 6 7 8 9 10
I have enough money.	1 2 3 4 5 6 7 8 9 10
My body is healthy.	1 2 3 4 5 6 7 8 9 10
I take time for my spirituality.	1 2 3 4 5 6 7 8 9 10
I feel good about the way I look.	1 2 3 4 5 6 7 8 9 10
I'm close to my significant other.	1 2 3 4 5 6 7 8 9 10
I'm close with my children.	1 2 3 4 5 6 7 8 9 10

I'm close with my parents.	1 2 3 4 5 6 7 8 9 10
I'm close with my siblings.	1 2 3 4 5 6 7 8 9 10
I take time for creative pursuits.	1 2 3 4 5 6 7 8 9 10
I have a balanced life.	1 2 3 4 5 6 7 8 9 10
I take time for exercise.	1 2 3 4 5 6 7 8 9 10
_____.	1 2 3 4 5 6 7 8 9 10
_____.	1 2 3 4 5 6 7 8 9 10

Your goal may be to experience every area of your life as a 10. Depending on where you are now, that may or may not be a realistic goal. As you glance at the numbers you circled above, which ones jump out at you as areas you really want to work on? Put a star next to those. Was there anything that surprised you as you went through the items? Any additional insight to help you feel motivated in a difficult area?

Your Intuition Journal

Don't use the exercise above or the journal question below as an opportunity to beat up on yourself! Simply observe that there are some areas that might need a bit more focus than others.

Here's your journal question:

How can I get to 10 on the areas that are important to me?

Think of small steps that would enable you to improve in these areas. You don't have to do this all at once. You might consider a time span of several months to several years to make some of these changes. Most important, remember to acknowledge your successes and achievements.

LESSON 21

———◈———

Living Your Dreams

I have found that you have only to take that one step towards the gods, and they will then take ten steps toward you.

—Joseph Campbell

Is there a part of your life that's stuck on hold because you're afraid to try something new? Have you found yourself getting so caught up in the frustrations of your job, driving your kids to their various after-school programs, making meals, struggling with life, that you forget to ask yourself, "What's my true purpose here?" Perhaps you're even afraid to have goals, hopes, dreams, and ambitions because you believe you have no way of achieving them, and you'd just be disappointed. Dr. Richard D. Dobbins stated it this way: "Until the pain of remaining the same hurts more than the pain of change, most people prefer to remain the same."

One of my first clients came into my office about twenty-five years ago. Helen was an older woman, well dressed and quite attractive. This lovely, gracious woman was terribly stuck in a rut. I remember trying to give her a reading. Every time I suggested a new or different way of approaching an issue or situation in her life, Helen would inform me as to why it wasn't possible!

She had quite a litany of excuses, all based on what she had learned about herself through psychoanalysis. "When I was four years old my mother forced toilet training on me, so therefore I don't like to try new things." Or "I couldn't learn a new skill. My father always told me I wasn't smart enough." Here was an intelligent woman totally stuck in the past. All of Helen's energy, thinking, and beliefs were focused on what had been before. When I asked her if she had any hopes for the future, she looked at me blankly and said, "I'm afraid to think of anything new. How do you begin?"

Your situation may not be as extreme as Helen's, but you may have the same question: How to begin? Here's the pattern that I find most people have when trying to create their dreams: 1) They're bored with what they have or what they're doing. 2) They decide they want to change or leave this situation. 3) They tap into their intuition and can usually describe a goal they have, or at least something they feel they have some enthusiasm about. 4) They wait. 5) Nothing happens. 6) They give up on their dream and decide that it wasn't "meant to be." Pretty depressing, isn't it?

The essential key missing from the above is that no *action* was taken. You can receive all the intuitive guidance in the world, but if you don't *act* on it, nothing will change. Taking action on your wishes and goals tells the Universe you're ready for your dream to come true. Susan Jeffers, author of the book *Feel the Fear and Do It Anyway*, suggests that you "take a risk a day—one small or bold stroke that will make you feel great once you have done it."

In order for me to begin my intuitive-reading business, I had to take action. In my case that meant taking an intuition-development class, talking to some people who gave readings for a living, and then getting the courage to actually give readings myself. I had to write a brochure about my services, tell a newspaper reporter I was a psychic, and then be willing to be interviewed by that reporter. You get the idea. I had to take action. Was I scared? *Yes!* But each time I took action I moved closer to my goal of a successful business, until it finally grew into reality.

My client Mary told me the other day that she felt she couldn't begin to take steps toward her dream until she felt better about herself. She explained that she suffered from low self-esteem. She added that she had prayed about this a lot and hadn't received an answer. My response was to point out that her inner guidance was trying to help her increase her confidence and self-respect by encouraging her to take action. She needed to begin to take baby steps toward her goals. Usually God doesn't appear with a handout of self-esteem. Instead he gives us the tools to dream, and the knowledge and wisdom to manifest those dreams. Your job is to listen. And love yourself enough to act.

Intuition Exercise: Dream Big!

Most people don't dream big enough. I want to get your "dreaming juices" flowing so you can follow your intuitive enthusiasms!

1. Write down in your journal at least five things that come quickly to mind after reading each of the following:

Places you'd like to visit:
Things you'd like to own:
Careers you've often dreamed about:
Famous people you'd like to meet:
Things you've always wanted to do:
Classes you've wanted to take:
Places you might want to live:
A description of your ideal vacation:
People you most admire and why:
A description of your dream house:

2. Next, go back through your list and circle four things that excite you the most. Write these down in your intuition journal.

3. What patterns or themes do you notice? (For example, they all have to do with taking a risk, or they have to do with creating a more relaxing pace in your life.)

The next step is what I call "information gathering." You don't have to figure out how you are going to reach your goal, you just have to ask for information. For example, if you've always dreamed about being involved in public relations, find someone who does it, call them, and request five minutes of their time to ask them questions about their career. If you have a love of photography, find out about classes in your area. Always wanted to visit Paris? Talk to a travel agent, or go to a library and check out some travel books.

4. Describe the information-gathering steps that you're willing to take toward helping you achieve the goals you wrote about in the third step.

Be willing to expand your information gathering a little further. You'll find that as you move in the direction of your goals and take appropriate risks, the Universe will begin to move with you, placing helpful people, synchronicities, and situations in your path. Your wise inner guidance placed those dreams in your heart and mind in the first place. By taking action *you're* helping the Universe *help you!*

Your Intuition Journal

Sometimes it's helpful to look at your past to better understand the successful coping skills that have allowed you to arrive where you are today.

Describe three things you're proud of achieving.
What obstacles did you have to overcome to achieve these?

It's also helpful to look at your present situation and directly address your fears so they don't sabotage your future success.

What's your biggest fear as you think about pursuing your goals?

What's the worst thing that could happen?

You may find yourself dwelling on your fears; I'd like you to focus, instead, on your potential for success.

What's the best thing that could happen?

What qualities do you have that will assist you in moving in the direction of your dreams, despite your fear? For example: persistence, integrity, faith, confidence, organization, sense of humor.

LESSON 22

———◆———

Put the Focus on Your Joy

*I firmly believe the universe dreams a bigger dream for
you than you can dream for yourself. . . . You've got
to open yourself to the dream that the universe has for
you. . . . You've got to discover your true calling.*

—Oprah Winfrey

Do you often awake to a new day tired, filled with dread, and lacking enthusiasm for what lies ahead? Perhaps you've grown to resent your job, or you're constantly annoyed with your spouse, or you snap at your kids. If this sounds like your life then you're probably ignoring some very important messages from your inner self. It's time to pay attention.

There *is* a way out of this situation. It will take some courage, commitment, and persistence. It may not happen overnight, so it will require patience as well. The answer begins within you. You deserve a life you love. You *can* have a life that is filled with joy and enthusiasm. You probably wish that there was a secret magic trick I could offer, or that I could tell you how to change your life in five easy steps. But it's not so simple. You need to do some work. Your job is to figure out what makes you joyful. That is the key to beginning to understand your true calling. I know that many of you reading this are already groaning, "If I knew that, I'd be doing it!" However, let's look at the reality here—who else has the answer except you? No one can rescue you from your current situation. It begins with you.

You have within you a powerful inner guidance system. It's hard-wired into you and it connects you to Divine intelligence, or God. If you are living a life in which you constantly feel drained, ener-vated, and depressed, you've shut off the current of energy from the vital source—your inner wisdom. Your task is to begin to reclaim the connection.

Here is a universal truth: *What you focus on expands*. Being truly honest with yourself, answer this question: What have you been focusing on? I'd be willing to bet that your attention hasn't been on gratitude, appreciation, and joy. You may not see the immediate connection between what goes on in your mind and your lack of energy, your lousy job, or your irritation with your spouse. But I assure that you it does exist, and for now you may have to accept this on faith.

Focus your emotions on the simple joys that are present in your life—family, good health, a beautiful day, a wet kiss from your puppy, or a hug from a child. Finding "joy" in life's events can be a difficult challenge, but it is well worth the effort. Take time to tune in to your inner voice; be still and listen. Begin to ask the questions, What makes me feel joyful? What do I have in my life that I feel good about? What do I like about me? What do I like about my family, my work, and my home? You'll know you've got the right feeling when you begin to experience that buzz of excite-ment, or a deep sense of calm and inner peace. Beginning to pay attention to your "joy feelings" is a first step toward creating a life you love. Remember: *What you focus on expands . . .*

Intuition Exercise:
Utilizing the Power of Your Beliefs

Your beliefs about your life give shape to how your life unfolds. What are some of your major beliefs? Your beliefs will be reflected back to you in your daily life. They produce what you experience. Answer the questions in the following list. If it's helpful, write the answers in your intuition journal.

Do you believe:

> Life has to be a struggle?
> It's possible for you to be happy?
> You live in a safe world?
> You will find joy in life?
> It's important to suffer?

What other core beliefs do you have about your life and the world at large? You may find that as you listen to and act on your inner wisdom, you begin to experience more peace and less anxiety and stress.

Your Intuition Journal

It's unfortunately become a dominant part of our culture to whine and complain. If you accept the idea that you create more of what you concentrate on, go against the tide! A great way to increase your well-being is to put your focus on what is currently working well in your life.

> What makes you feel joy-filled?
> What do you have in your life that you feel good about?
> What do you like about yourself?
> What do you like about your family?
> What do you like about your work?
> What do you like about your home?
> What could you do to increase joy in your life?

As you answered the questions, you may have discovered that many areas in your life are not *all* good or *all* bad. For instance, you may say that you "hate your job" but also realize that you like the people you work with and the fact that you have flexible hours. Again, as you place your focus on what you like and enjoy, you'll find those aspects expanding in your life.

LESSON 23

⸺ ◈ ⸺

The Power of Positive Attraction

*We are each responsible for our lives and, more important,
the thoughts that create them. If you want your life to be
more rewarding, you have to change the way you think.*

—Oprah Winfrey

What you say when you talk to yourself has a huge impact on what happens in your life. You create your focus through the power of your thoughts and the images you hold in your mind and emotions. When you begin to choose your thoughts in a more conscious fashion, you can begin to shape your destiny.

How is your intuition tied into this? When you are consistently holding negative or pessimistic thoughts, you will feel bad. This is one of the ways your intuition has of signaling you that you're on the wrong track. It's as if your bad mood or irritability is your intuition's early-warning system letting you know you're about to create something less than positive in your life. It's cautioning you to redirect your thinking.

Try this experiment:

Think of something you really want. Got it? Now spend about thirty seconds saying to yourself, "I'll never get it. I'm not good enough. I'm not lucky. It will never happen." You get the idea.

Now how do you feel? Pretty crummy, right? Great! Your intuition was giving you a message to change your thinking!

Try this again. Bring to mind what you want to create in your life. Spend thirty seconds saying, "I'm so excited about having this [name the thing or achievement]. I know I'm on the right track. I have what it takes to succeed at this. It's only a matter of time until it happens." I'll bet you feel more positive. Again, this is a message from your intuition. This time your good feelings are an indication that you're on the right track and are sending out the right vibration or energy to attract what you desire. The spiritual teacher Ron Rathbun said it best when he stated, "What you find in your mind is what you put there. Put good things in there."

Intuition Exercise:
Accentuate the Positive

Pay attention to your thoughts and feelings. If you catch yourself feeling down, depressed, or just plain pessimistic, see if you can redirect your thoughts back to what you were just thinking about or telling yourself.

Be vigilant about turning your negative thoughts into something positive. Notice that when you get feedback from your intuition, it indicates the thoughts you're thinking are not attracting what you desire. Then immediately ask yourself these two questions:

1. What do I want in this situation?
2. Is there a more positive way of thinking about it?

Continue to choose thoughts that make you feel better. This doesn't mean that I'm asking you to lie to yourself. I'm asking you to choose a thought that feels better. I want you to be compassionate with yourself as you learn this new skill. It takes practice to be a conscious creator of your world!

Your Intuition Journal

Write about some of the negative things you say to yourself on a regular basis. What would be a more positive way of viewing the situation? Look at the examples below. Then write your "turn-arounds" by asking, "What thought feels better?" Choose one positive thought you'd really like to focus on each week.

Negative things I say to myself on a regular basis:	Positive turnarounds:
I have really bad luck.	I'm learning that my thoughts create my luck and I'm willing to think more positively.
I'll never be rich.	There are many areas in my life in which I experience abundance. I know I'll be able to create enough money as well.
Write your examples in your journal.	

One of the ways to catch yourself at making negative statements is to become aware of saying things like, "I always . . . ," I never . . . ," I'm not good at . . . ," or "With my terrible luck, I . . ." As with any bad habit, with practice and conscious attention, you can change. I guarantee that if you do, you'll change your life as a result.

LESSON 24

—◆◆◆—

Wired to Infinite Intelligence

*The intuitive mind has access to an infinite
supply of information. It is able to tap into a deep
storehouse of knowledge and wisdom—the universal
mind. It is also able to sort out this information and
supply us with exactly what we need, when we need it.
Our role is to listen to our intuition, trust its guidance,
and learn to act on it step by step in our lives.*

—Shakti Gawain

Every moment of every day, you receive information about whether
you are on course or off course. This information comes from your
finely tuned spiritual radar, called "your intuition," and if heeded,
it can make sure you're headed in the direction of your dreams.

I've often thought of inner guidance as being broadcast from an
infinite intelligence. I liken it to a stream of radio waves. They're
invisible. You can't see or hear them unless you make an effort to
tune in. Make a daily effort to lock onto station WISE.

Developing intuition is like learning any new skill or talent.
The more you practice it, the better you get at it. Over time you
become attuned to the Divine Intuition frequency, which allows
you to hear the broadcast that directs you toward the right path.

It's not so different from perfecting other skills. I love to cook. I know that the addition of a certain combination of spices can make my dish a success or a disaster. So I pay attention to the feedback from my sense of taste to know whether I'm on the right track.

It's the same with intuition. You can begin to pay attention to the subtle nudge, inner voice, or gentle stirrings that make up the combination of ingredients that go into your personal mix of inner guidance. When you develop your abilities through asking questions and staying alert to the gentle inner promptings of your guidance, your life begins to change.

A woman named Megan recently sent me a note and put it this way: "I no longer feel alone in the world. I understand now that the thoughts and ideas that make me feel excited and glad to be alive are part of my intuitive guidance system. They show me the way to my life purpose. It's as if there is a kind friend and mentor out there in the Universe who supports my dream. My job is to dream that dream big enough and be willing to take the necessary steps to make it happen. I receive information about how to do that through my intuition."

I think Megan is on to an important truth. Many of us harbor the fear that we're not doing "God's will" if we simply move in the direction of our dreams and passions. Julia Cameron writes in *The Artist's Way*, "We are not accustomed to thinking that God's will for us and our own inner dreams can coincide." It sounds too easy and somehow superficial. How do you know when what you are doing is part of your life purpose, your mission, or, to put it in more Christian terms, God's will?

I believe we were given a guidance system or set of inner instructions to help us stay on course and understand our soul's journey on earth. It makes sense that if you feel bad, guilty, or filled with fear, if you lack energy or are chronically worried about a situation, these indications should be taken as feedback that you're off track somewhere in your life. Conversely, if you are feeling good and in general your life is filled with small joys, hope, productive work, good friends, and a sense of purpose, you're on track.

Be willing to accept the possibility that you are being guided each step along the way. You are not alone. God wants you to be happy, to live a life of joy, love, and hope. Pay attention to the wise guidance available to help you find your path. Remember to ask for help. You are tuned in to an infinite intelligence that broadcasts love, acceptance, and wisdom, and is there to shine light on your path—step by step. Your greatest desire is always God's wish for you. Breathe deeply, let go, trust, tune in, have faith, and keep moving.

Intuition Exercise: Daily Intuitive Review

Before you go to bed at night, conduct an intuitive review of the day. Close your eyes, bring back the high points of your day, and answer the following questions before you drift off to sleep.

What were you doing today when you felt most at peace?

How could you structure your life in order to do more of that?

Was there any time when you felt uncomfortable? (Anxious, worried, out of the flow?)

If yes, what could you have done differently?

When you wake up in the morning, here are some questions to think about:

What are you looking forward to today?

Is there anything you're anxious about?

If yes, how would you like the situation to go? Spend a few moments visualizing a successful outcome.

What one thing could you accomplish that will make you feel good about the day?

Asking yourself these questions on a regular basis helps you move your life in the right direction. Intuition gives you very simple directions at times: move away from what drains you and move toward what gives you energy.

Your Intuition Journal

Have you ever been stuck in a situation where it appears that the only chance you have of experiencing happiness or relief is if the other person would change and simply agree with your point of view? You might be in that situation at work with a difficult boss, or perhaps you feel unhappy because your spouse refuses to see things your way. Because you have no control over another person, the path to your happiness will often lie in the direction of an inner shift in your own thinking.

What are the situations in your life that you feel angry or resentful about?

Is there a shift in your thinking that would allow you to experience some peace of mind regarding this person or situation?

What are you willing to do about it?

What are the situations where you experienced peace or happiness?

How can you increase the time you spend in these situations?

Begin to think along these lines: "If the other person or situation does not change, what could I do to experience peace?" Just asking yourself that question may open you to intuitive answers and a new, more productive direction.

Small Steps to Big Dreams

Try saying the phrase, "Let me be open to the possibilities."
Just be open—there is no commitment to action. . . .
Saying this phrase to yourself a few times a day
opens your heart to intuitive feelings.

—Nancy Rosanoff

Yesterday I spoke with a client I'll call Barbara. She began the session with a barrage of complaints about her life and her job. "I don't like the people I work with. I'm not paid enough for what I do, and I hate my job." My attempts at interjecting any helpful insights, questions, or guidance were met with another barrage of what wasn't working in her life. A line from Richard Bach kept going through my mind: "If you argue in favor of your limitations, you get to keep them." Finally, in a less than patient fashion, I said, "Barbara, if you don't stop whining you're going to add an unhelpful session with me to the list of things you can complain about." I couldn't believe I had said that! It stopped her cold.

When we both recovered, I asked as kindly as possible, "What would your life look like if you had what you wanted?" She started to list all the impediments to creating something new in her life; then she paused. "I don't know what I want," she said in a small voice. "Everyone seems to have big dreams, and I gave up on mine a long time ago. I have no idea what to do anymore."

Barbara's situation may sound a bit extreme, but I know that many people have a difficult time identifying their goals. One of the questions I'm asked most frequently is, "What's my purpose in life?" Many books and classes out there claim to help you make your dreams come true, but what if you seem to have no big objectives or aspirations? Your intuition can help you in a significant way with this dilemma.

Your inner guidance continually informs you about your life purpose through things and events that make you happy. Paying attention to these is the first step in beginning to create a larger dream. When you take one step in the direction of saying "yes" to what you love, the Universe rushes in with help, guidance, and miracles. Here are some questions to get you started:

> What are you doing when time seems to fly by?
> What do you look forward to doing on the weekends or on a vacation?
> Think of someone who has a "dream job"—what do they do?
> If money were no object, what kind of work would you love to do?
> If your boss told you she'd give you a year off to contribute to the community in some way, what would you choose to do?
> What are your hobbies?

I realize that the answer to any of those questions is not necessarily going to evoke instant clarity about either your vocation or your life mission, but it's a start. Every single person who is living a life they love had to begin by asking themselves these questions. They also had to believe in themselves enough to take the risks to move in the direction of their dreams. You don't need to quit your day job right now, but simply begin spending more time doing what you love. Reach out to make connections with others who might be able to help you with creating your dream, and continue to dream a little bigger with each day.

Remember that life can be easy. There isn't any great virtue in struggling and suffering. Begin to ask the question, "How could I...?" rather than "Why can't I?" If your heart and mind are open to the limitless possibilities that God can provide, all you seek will begin to flow smoothly into your life.

When you tap into the Universe and ask for assistance in understanding and realizing your dreams, miraculous events may begin to occur. Information about your life purpose will fill your thoughts and fuel your actions. Impediments such as low self-esteem and anxiety will diminish, and maybe even fall away, leaving your aspirations free to emerge and gain strength. Little by little, step by step, a new life will begin to take shape. Have faith and courage, and listen to the voice of God's wisdom within you. Then begin to act on the insight you receive.

Intuition Exercise:
Connecting Through Meditation

Look at some of the answers you came up with to the questions listed above. It's important to ask your intuition for help in creating your dream. You have unlimited sources to assist you on your path to achieving your goals. You may want to play some soothing music that will create a feeling of reverence.

- Close your eyes and inhale deeply and then exhale slowly, observing your breath as it goes in and out of your body.
- As you continue to breathe, envision yourself being bathed in a soft white light. (Pause.)
- Imagine yourself moving upward into a higher realm. There is no right or wrong way to imagine this. Just intend for it to happen and it will.

- The space around you is full of love and compassion. Spend a few minutes allowing the light and love to expand. Allow these images and feelings to flow through you and all around you.
- When you feel ready, here are some questions to ask your intuition:
    "What am I here to learn?"
    "What is my life purpose?"
    "What next steps should I take to further my life purpose?"
    "How can I develop my intuition?"
    "How can I create more peace and balance in my life?"
    "Is there anything that is blocking me from achieving my goals?"
- Ask any other questions that you want insight about.
- Stay in the meditation for as long as you like. When you're ready, come back to normal consciousness and open your eyes.
- Take out your notebook and write down the guidance you received. Record any thoughts, physical sensations, or images.

Some people report that they receive answers to questions while writing about the experience, not when they're in the middle of meditation. Others report that the answers come in their dreams at night. Don't be discouraged if the intuitive responses did not come during the exercise. It works differently for everyone. The important thing is to make the attempt to connect with your intuition and the Universe through the meditation process. Sometimes, even when nothing appears to be going on, there is a lot of information being transferred on an unconscious level. The Divine knowledge you seek may pop into your mind when you least expect it!

Your Intuition Journal

The actress Katharine Hepburn once stated, in her inimitable style, "Life is to be lived. If you have to support yourself, you had bloody well better find some way that is going to be interesting. And you don't do that by sitting around wondering about yourself." If that statement doesn't get you moving, I don't know what else will! Here are some questions to get you started:

> List three things you love to do.
> What typically prevents you from doing these things more often?
> Do you believe that doing these fun things will move you closer to a life you love?

If you answered yes, write the following statement in your journal, and sign your name to it. You're making a commitment to join forces with the Universe to create a life you love—one step at a time.

I, [your name], commit to doing more of what I love this week and in the weeks to come.

Think of having more fun as a "homework assignment from your soul." You may be surprised at how play, frivolity, entertainment, and general amusement can become both habit forming and life affirming!

LESSON 26

—◆—

Embrace All of Life's Offerings

I keep the telephone of my mind open to peace, harmony,
health, love, and abundance. Then, whenever doubt,
anxiety, or fear try to call me, they will keep getting
a busy signal—and soon they'll forget my number.

—Edith Armstrong

"I hate detours!" I exclaimed to a friend the other day as we found ourselves caught in a traffic jam. "Isn't it a perfect spring day?" she responded as she rolled down the car window, leaned back, and sighed. That's the difference between my friend and me. I'm a bit driven. I want to get from here to there in the quickest way possible. She, however, manages to at least enjoy the journey.

This was one of those "Aha" moments that made me more aware of a pattern I've been trying to break. I see it in myself and so many of my friends and clients; it's the plague of rushing, busyness, anxiety, and stress. What's the big hurry?!

Remember to check in with your inner guidance when you feel anxious. This feeling of hurry is self-imposed, and it's possible to shift it so you can feel more relaxed and in the flow of life. I used to think of spiritual practice as going to church, meditating for a half hour, or reading a book on prayer. It can include all those things, and yet for me it means taking the risk to trust the

Universe—to slow down and savor life. It is all unfolding at its own pace.

I focus on the present moment, taking a deep breath. I'm aware that even as I've been writing these words, I'm rushing. My intention was to finish this chapter this morning—self-imposed pressure. I breathe in again and I'm aware of a bird singing in the trees near my office. I notice the sun through the skylight brightening the fresh yellow daisies on my desk. I look out the window and see the beginnings of new growth on the old trees. I open the window and enjoy the cool breeze as it plays with my hair. I have paused for just a few moments, halted the jumble of harsh thoughts urging me to finish my writing for the day. I am reminded of a Zen poem: "Sitting quietly, doing nothing / Spring comes and grass grows by itself."

Simple.
Stop for a moment.
Breathe.
Focus.
Check in with Spirit.
Appreciate.
Slow down.
Begin again.
Ahh . . .
(I could love life like this.)

Intuition Exercise:
Take a Life-Balance Break

Become aware of moments when you're feeling anxious, stressed, and hurried. Your task is to begin to break the pattern and allow flow, ease, and openness into your life.

Here are some tools to use. Take what works for you and discard the rest.

When you think about your week, what were the times that were most stressful?

What could you do to change that?

List five things you enjoyed during the previous week. How could you incorporate those moments into your life on a regular basis?

We all have a long list of things we are "supposed to do" to assist us on our path to health in mind, body, and spirit. Most of us don't do these things because they require too much time. We then spend a great deal of energy beating ourselves up for not doing them. What are five things you would like to incorporate into your life? (For example, meditation, journal writing, prayer, yoga, walking, or dancing.) Instead of not doing them at all, give yourself permission to do them for five minutes a day.

Set the timer on your computer or watch to go off every hour. Take a Spirit break. Go for a brief walk, stand up and stretch, go outside and smell the roses, play with your kids, call a friend and tell them you love them. Do something that brings you back to the present moment in your life.

There is no one *right way* to get to where you want to go. Ask your Spirit how you can enjoy all of what life offers you. Remember to savor life; enjoy the detours.

Your Intuition Journal

Don't *think* about these questions too much. Just write what immediately comes to your mind:

When did you have the most fun . . .

> in the past week?
> in the past month?
> in the past year?

Write these words in your journal:

I give myself permission to have more fun.

Forget being so serious about your spiritual path, your job, your relationship, your weight, your skills as a parent, your health, or whether you're doing something "right" or as well as someone else. Take some time off from trying to "create a life you love" and just simply go enjoy it. Who else is going to enjoy your life if you don't?!

LESSON 27

―◉―

Which Thought Feels Better?

The Universe totally supports every thought
I choose to think and believe. I have unlimited
choices about what I think. I choose balance,
harmony, and peace, and I express it in my life.

—Louise Hay

Last month I was teaching a class called Creating a Life You Love. I was going over the lesson about affirmations. I stated something I thought was self-evident—that each of us has an internal dialogue going on at all times, and in essence we're constantly talking to ourselves. A man sitting to my right let out an audible gasp and exclaimed, "Oh! I'm so glad you said that. I thought I was the only one who talked to myself!"

Have you ever suddenly and inexplicably felt depressed or irritable when just moments before you'd felt fine? That happens to all of us from time to time. The next time it happens, take a moment to remember what occurred just prior to your shift in emotions. You'll likely come up with something someone said or did that hurt your feelings, or a situation that arose that made you feel bad in some way.

The important thing is to observe your thoughts. What did you tell yourself about the comment or situation that made you feel bad? Learning to ask this question whenever you experience a sudden mood shift is vitally important. You'll have some instant insight into some core thoughts and beliefs.

I'll give you an example to illustrate this point. Recently I was coaching Roy, a middle manager at a corporation near Boston. We were speaking about his recent successes and an award that he had received the week before. He was upbeat and positive as we spoke.

Moving on to a different subject, I asked him something about his boss, Neil. Roy immediately began shifting in his seat. His energy and posture changed, and he looked crestfallen. I was startled by the abrupt shift and asked, "What did you just tell yourself about the topic of Neil?" He quickly replied, "I'll never be as smart as Neil. I won't get ahead because I'm not as good as him." I remarked that it was interesting to me that we could be talking about his successes one moment, then make such a rapid shift in focus based on his self-defeating internal dialogue.

Clearly it didn't help Roy to perceive himself as unintelligent and incapable of getting ahead. Neither was it true! The rest of the session was spent in reframing how he saw himself in relation to others. The next time he experienced the beginning of a negative thought pattern, he learned to question it and ask, "What's a more productive way of thinking about this?" The answer he came up with in connection to his boss was to say to himself, "I have many abilities that enable me to do my job well. They are just a different set of skills than Neil's."

The book A Course in Miracles has an affirmation that says, "I could choose peace instead of this." You have a choice about the thoughts you pay attention to. You can choose the ones that make you feel good, hopeful, and positive or the ones that make you feel rotten, hopeless, and miserable. Take a look at how this model works in the Intuition Exercise.

Intuition Exercise:
Find Reasons to Feel Good

Begin to look for reasons to feel good, and consciously change the direction of your thoughts. Practice asking your inner guidance, "Is there another way to view this situation?" and listen for the answers. Here's a practice exercise:

Write a few sentences about a recent event that you felt bad about.

What did you say to yourself about this situation? How did you interpret what took place?

What is another way of viewing or interpreting the situation that makes you feel better?

Here's an example from my journal:

The situation: I had a miscommunication with a local landscaper about the cost of planting some bushes in our backyard. I realized that this was my misinterpretation of the work involved. It was not his fault.

My interpretation/what I told myself: I spent the day feeling bad because I felt I had spent too much money. I was chastising myself for not keeping to our budget. I began generalizing that I was not good at saving money. I told myself that I should be investing that money in our retirement fund.

An alternate way of viewing the situation: I began to stop beating myself up when I asked the question, "How can I look at this differently?" The answers came flooding into my mind. I feel expansive when I look into my "new" backyard. I feel good that I could afford to have this work done. I trust that more money will come from some other source to more than make up for this money I spent.

Epilogue: The next day my husband received a contract for his freelance work that more than covered the check I'd just written to the landscaper. I find over and over again that when I can shift my thinking to feeling good about something and placing my focus on what I want rather than what I don't want, I create positive results. Ask your intuition to direct your thinking. Your inner wisdom will always guide you to well-being.

Your Intuition Journal

Do you have a chronic situation in your life that takes a lot of your energy? This might be an area in which you are disappointed, sad, or discouraged.

Write one or two sentences about this situation in your journal.

What do you tell yourself about this situation?

For example: "This will never change." "I'm just not good at this."

What could you tell yourself that would make you feel better and more optimistic?

For example: "This situation is only temporary." "I'm taking steps to change and this will get better." "I've been in difficult situations before and things have worked out."

What are you willing to do to change your internal dialogue to be more positive?

Sometimes you may not feel that you have options, or you may believe that the other person or the situation has power and you have none. This is rarely true, and continuing to think that way may shut you off from your wise inner guidance attempting to offer you solutions. Answers and options will come to your mind and heart. Allow yourself to be open to the potential for change.

LESSON 28

———◦◉◦———

Transforming Your Fear

*We cannot escape fear. We can transform it into a
companion that accompanies us on all our exciting
adventures. . . . Take a risk a day—one small or bold
stroke that will make you feel great once you have done it.*

—Susan Jeffers

Divine intuition speaks to you most strongly through your hopes
and dreams. God communicates your next steps through what you
feel excited and passionate about. In talking to thousands of
clients, I've discovered that many of us suppress and restrain our
enthusiasm. Have you ever done that? You might have been excited
about a work project, a potential move, a new business venture,
but you talked yourself out of it. You let your initial enthusiasm
fade away.

Many of us do that because the task seems insurmountable. How
do I get from Point A (where I am) to Point B (where I want to
be)? The Roman philosopher Seneca stated, "It is not because
things are difficult that we do not dare; it is because we do not
dare that they are difficult." We give up when our fear gets in our
way. Intuition can provide you with the appropriate steps to take
to bring your dream to fruition.

Intuition Exercise:
Small Steps, Big Gains

1. Think of a goal or dream you've had. Write it in your journal.

Examples:

I'd like to lose twenty pounds.
I want to be self-employed in my own graphic-design business.
I want to be a well-known poet.
I'd love to be a great watercolorist.

2. Each morning when you arise and each evening before going to bed, visualize yourself having achieved your goal. Just spend a few minutes each time.

3. Think of a small step you could take that would move you toward your goal. Think of something you feel excited about that doesn't feel like too much of a stretch to achieve.

Examples:

I'd like to lose four pounds this month.
I'd like to find out more about starting a business.
I'd like to discover where I could read my poetry in public.
I'd like to find a great watercolor class.

4. Begin to take the small steps you listed above. Each day, pay attention to what you feel enthusiastic about in relation to your goal. This is your intuition communicating with you and encouraging you toward your goal. Take action on your enthusiasms!

Your Intuition Journal

Creating major change in your life can feel overwhelming. Many people *don't* change, if given an option. They prefer to stay stuck and wait until they're assured that the change they contemplate will be successful. Those assurances are rarely forthcoming, and then it's often too late. Think of the excitement and enthusiasm you feel as your intuition indicating the direction of some *small* steps to take.

What do you feel excited about today?
What small steps can you take toward your goal?

Your action plan:
Success breeds success. As you start to take small steps, you'll feel more self-confident and you'll develop trust that your intuition will lead you in the right direction. Slowly but surely you'll find that you'll experience a greater sense of self-achievement and satisfaction.

LESSON 29

— ⏥ —

Angels as God's Messengers

*We're not that difficult to hear, if you will listen for us
with an open heart. Most of the time, we are closer to
you than you can imagine. A whisper, a thought, is the
only signal we need from you to get a conversation
started. We have enormous respect for what you're going
through here on planet Earth at this time. We never seek
to interfere with your lives, only to bring you blessings
of insights and new ways of looking at yourselves.*

—Angel message as quoted by Doreen Virtue

When I was a child, I had an angel that tucked me in every night before I went to sleep. I called her "the Lady." She always stood at the foot of my bed. I never actually saw her, but I could *feel* her presence. I envisioned her as radiating golden light. I would imagine her wings embracing me and sending such pure love and joy that I would fall asleep feeling surrounded by her radiance. Now, no longer a child, I still seek her out, asking her for guidance and direction in meditation.

The word *angel* is derived from the Greek word *angelos*, which means messenger. Angels are often mentioned in literature as intermediaries between God and humans. They are celestial beings that communicate with you through many of the same means from which you receive intuitive information—feelings, words, images, sounds, and physical sensations.

One of the questions I'm frequently asked is, "How do you tell the difference between messages from your intuition, your guides, and your angels?" My short answer is "Practice." My long answer is that if the information you receive is helpful, assists you in making good decisions, and allows you to lead your life in a loving and productive manner, it really doesn't matter what the source is.

Angels are sometimes confused with "spirit guides." A spirit guide is a loving being who has had an incarnation in physical form. We all have a guide who is there to give us advice, comfort, spiritual instruction, and, at times, protection. Your spirit guide could be a friend or a relative who has died. Your guide may also be a spiritually advanced soul who is acting as your mentor to help you with a difficult time in your life, or with a specific endeavor such as being a good parent, or with a creative project. I believe you are also assigned one special guide who is with you throughout your entire life.

My experience is that guides are often more predictive with their information, offering concrete advice and counsel. When you experience a communication from an angel, the love you feel is tangible. People often report these experiences as characterized by feelings of greater self-acceptance, inner peace, and a sense of being deeply cared for and cherished.

Angels have been with us forever. There are representations of angels in every culture and religion, throughout history. In the past decade we are once again hearing about angels. I believe they are making more consistent contact with us because more and more of us are open to their healing influence.

When my angel is present, I get powerful feelings of love, joy, and hope. Others have reported a physical sensation similar to being hugged, or a fleeting impression of a breeze. Still others say they hear a loving whisper or a sound of celestial music being played before they get an angelic message. There is no *right way* or *wrong way* to receive a message from your angel. When you feel that an angel is present, just trust that it's so.

Intuition Exercise:
Chatting with Your Angel

My favorite method of communicating with my angels is simply to sit quietly with pen and paper at hand. I like to write the answers I receive because they are often profoundly beautiful and full of love, clarity, and appreciation. I also find it helpful to look back at the information I've received. I'm frequently surprised at how accurate and insightful the comments are. Musician Stephen Halpern has a wonderful CD called *Gifts of the Angels*. Listening to his music puts me in the perfect mood for the following meditation.

- Find a time when you won't be interrupted. Turn off the ringer on your phone and simply sit quietly. Close your eyes and take a deep breath. Bring your thoughts and feelings into quiet harmony. Imagine that you are readying your heart and mind for an important spiritual visitor. Your intention is to be fully present and alert, yet open and receptive.
- Imagine that you are surrounded by light. See it flowing all around you and connected to all the love in the Universe. Visualize streams of light coming from the heavens and coursing through your entire being. Imagine that you are connecting with this light and feel yourself opening to it. You might imagine that you are floating among the stars. Spend a few minutes with this image.
- Shift your focus to your heart. Take a deep breath and exhale slowly. Observe and sense the love that is filling you and is all around you. Feel your angel's presence wanting to communicate with you.
- Ask your angel a question. Take whatever issue pops into your mind first. Here's a list of questions you might want to ask:

"How can I stay in contact with you?"
"What should I call you?"

"How do you want to work with me?"
"What message do you have for me?"
"What do I need right now?"
"What's my purpose in life?"

• You may feel an emotion and then find words forming in your mind. Trust whatever you receive. Your angel may also communicate through images or pictures.

• When you feel ready, open your eyes and begin to write the words or draw the images. Write whatever comes to you. Don't censor what you receive. Just continue to be open and let go of any judgment.

• As with any conversation, you'll have more questions as you receive answers. Continue to talk back and forth until you feel complete. When you're done, thank your angel and read over what you have received.

• People often feel that they have "made up" the answer. Communicating with angels makes you feel as if you are operating on a higher frequency. If the presence you experienced felt calm, loving, and compassionate, trust that you were hearing the voice of your angel. Angel communications run the gamut from funny and simple to extraordinarily wise and inspiring. They always offer a positive view or loving advice.

• As you come back into your body and take in your surroundings, it's time to evaluate. Ask yourself what you learned. How did it make you feel? Was the information helpful and correct? As with all new skills, practice helps! You may want to try again immediately or simply put the information away for a while and revisit it in a few weeks or months.

Your Intuition Journal

Angels often bring help and guidance in unexpected ways, but you have to ask for help first!

List five things you would like your angels to help you with.

What was the most helpful piece of information you received from your angels?

Always remember to thank your angels for their assistance. After all, they appreciate acknowledgment just like humans!

LESSON 30

Plug into Your Power

I trust inner Wisdom as it guides my choices. There is within me that which knows the best choice for me now, including the choice to be still and listen and wait. Every day, love sparkles in my experiences. Love goes forth from me to all people.

—Reverend Mary Murray Shelton

I've been doing intuitive consulting for over twenty years. It's still amazing to me how some people are able to transform their lives while others stay in a rut year after year. I've thought long and hard about what allows some people to lead successful, happy, and balanced lives. Here are the keys that I've observed.

Successful people . . .

. . . have a clear dream or goal. They pay attention to what makes them happy, enthusiastic, and energized. They use that information to assist them in making the right choices and decisions.

. . . visualize and affirm their success. Not all of them sit down and formally focus on visualizations and affirmations. They picture their dreams and in their own internal dialogue they affirm their ability to achieve their goals.

. . . trust their intuition. Whether they call it a hunch, an instinct, or Divine guidance, they pay attention to their inner voice.

They take action on the information that their intuition provides and follow its wisdom.

. . . take appropriate risks. They understand that they'll have to move out of their comfort zone at times and risk doing something unfamiliar. They know that everyone feels nervous and anxious when attempting something new. Despite this discomfort, they persevere.

. . . have patience and faith. To achieve their goals they have a long-term perspective. They know they'll achieve what they desire. They enjoy the process of getting there as much as achieving the goal. They understand that there will be tough times, but they keep at it.

. . . trust that things will work out. They tell themselves that while they might be going through a difficult transition, they have what it takes to succeed. They focus on any and all successes they had in the past as evidence that points to this truth.

. . . take action. They understand that small steps are important. They have a plan. If they meet with a detour or an impediment in their path, they simply step back and reassess the situation. They discover where they may have gone wrong and proceed to take action again, this time in the right direction.

Intuition Exercise: Dwell on Your Successes

Many people choose a "half-empty-glass" view of life. They focus on all the things they haven't achieved. Spend some time writing about and dwelling on your successes. Think about the big ones, but, more important, recognize and acknowledge the small achievements. Here are some things to think about when considering your past successes:

> How did you know you were on track to meet your goals?
> Did you sense it in your body?
> Was it an instinct or a gut feeling?

Did you have a feeling or an image that indicated that you were moving in the right direction?

Were there synchronicities or coincidences that seemed to indicate that you were headed in the right direction?

Here are some things to consider when working with your present goals:

Do you feel energized and excited about what you want to do? If so, this is a signal from your intuition that you should continue.

Are things falling into place? If so, continue! If not, proceed slowly. Step back a bit and ask for guidance to see if a slight change in direction is needed.

Remember that things take time. Just because your goal isn't happening overnight doesn't mean it isn't going to happen. As a friend once said, "God's delays are not his denials." Be patient. Look for indications of success.

Are you having fun while trying to reach your goal? It's important to enjoy your life in the present moment as well as savoring your achievements. Once you've achieved a goal, you're usually on to the next one anyway, so take pleasure in the process!

Meditate and consult your Higher Power. Make time each week to spend some quiet time conversing with your soul about what you hope to achieve. Be still and listen as your spirit whispers encouragement, patience, and compassion.

Your Intuition Journal

Do you believe that the only way to reach your goals is to take a huge leap of faith? Anecdotal evidence from many successful people would prove otherwise. They would tell you that small changes were an equally important key to reaching their objectives.

What are three small changes you could make to help you feel more successful?

What risk have you taken in the past that had a positive outcome?

What small risk have you been secretly wanting to take?

Are you willing to do it? If not, why not?

What could you do this week that is new and different?

Consider forming a small support group of friends and colleagues to meet on a regular basis. Your intention would be to encourage one another to take the necessary steps to create the goals each of you wish to achieve.

LESSON 31

―――◆◉◆―――

Divine Decisions

Ask for what you need and want. Ask to be taught the right questions. Ask to be answered. Ask for the Divine Plan of your life to unfold through joy. Ask politely. Ask with passion. Ask with a grateful heart and you will be heard.

—Sarah Ban Breathnach

Most of us hate making big decisions. Should I leave this job? Would my life be better if I moved to another place? Is it time to end this relationship? We usually agonize over these issues for weeks, months, or even years. I've observed that left to their own devices, most people decide not to decide. They let "fate" take its course. What this actually means is that they don't make an active choice about what they want, and they simply let circumstances choose for them.

Most of us would agree that we shouldn't aspire to feeling upset, down, depressed, and out-of-balance. We're striving for a life of balance and peace, right?! My answer: yes and no. When your life feels out of kilter, it's not necessarily a bad thing. It's simply a message from your Higher Self that it's time to make a change. The problem comes if you ignore the warning and a crisis erupts. Your inner wisdom will always give you the appropriate clues to help you stay on track in your life.

My client Judy told me she hated her job in pharmaceutical sales. She was desperate to get out of it. She was hoping and praying for some direction about her "life purpose." She had a strong desire to find a position in catering sales at a resort or an elegant restaurant. She wished that something would happen that would allow her to leave her current position. Meanwhile, she felt that she was doing a terrible job and her boss would inevitably let her go. "Why aren't my prayers being answered?" she asked.

Judy and I talked for quite a while about what she expected when she prayed. The essence of her belief was that if she prayed "correctly" God would deem her worthy of a new job and someone would call and offer it to her. Does it happen that way in reality? Occasionally. More often we receive the answer through a shift in perception about a situation, a boost of courage, or new opportunities that show up.

As Judy and I talked further she mentioned that a neighbor who was in the restaurant business had stopped by several months ago. They'd talked about her interest in catering sales, and he'd jotted down a list of people she could call who could help her. When I asked her why she hadn't been in touch with any of his referrals, she said, "What if I decide to change my job and I don't like the new one?"

The answered prayer may be clear to you, but it wasn't to Judy. How many of us have been given an intuitive nudge to take a risk, make a decision, or pursue some action, and simply refused to budge out of fear and simple indecision? When you ask for guidance, you receive an answer. It doesn't always come in an obvious form. John D. Rockefeller III said, "The road to happiness lies in two simple principles: find what it is that interests you and that you can do well, and when you find it, put your whole soul into it—every bit of energy and ambition and natural ability you have." Courage is needed in order to shed a safe and predictable life. Learn to embrace the new, remain open to answers, and move forward with an open heart.

Intuition Exercise:
Creating an Abundance of Options

Think about something you're unhappy about. You may want to write about it in your journal.

If you could be granted any wish regarding this situation, what would you like to have happen?

Think about five options you have relative to this issue. (For example: You could choose to talk to someone, to leave, to stay, to ask for help or support, to pray, to not decide, to take a risk, to shift your attitude, to continue doing what you've always done, to take action, or all of the above.) Write about these in your journal.

Close your eyes and take a deep breath. Ask your intuition, "What is the best course of action to take?" Pause.

Think about all the options you've just written down. Does any one of them leap out as the best decision? If not, go deeper and ask the question again. A new answer may emerge.

Write the results in your journal.

What three small steps can you take that will move you in the direction you've chosen? Give yourself a deadline of a day, a week, or a month to accomplish your next steps and go for it!

Your Intuition Journal

Not all people make successful decisions in the same way. There's no *one* right way. Spend some time thinking about the decision-making style that has worked for you in the past. If you can apply that information to your present decision, you'll have a head start in the right direction.

In your journal, describe three major decisions you've made in the past.

How do you typically make decisions? (For example: Stall until you can't stand it anymore? Let someone else decide? Trust your intuition and wait for the right time? Decide prematurely and perhaps create a crisis?)

Is your decision-making style successful for you?

If not, what would you like to change?

If yes, what makes it successful?

After answering these questions, you might decide to choose a different decision-making style. That's great! Use your new method in some low-risk situations at first, while you get comfortable with this new process.

LESSON 32

———◦❦◦———

Achieving Results

Imagination is everything. It is the
preview of life's coming attractions.

—Albert Einstein

Goal + imagination + positive emotions + intuition + action = the results you desire in your life. That's the simple formula. Let's break it down. What's your goal or intention? What is it that you want to create? How would you like your life to be different? Clearly define the outcome you desire. Many people get hung up at this stage and become fixated on *how* they'll achieve their goal. Attempt to put that concern aside for the next few weeks. Try this formula as an experiment in how to create something new in your life. For now, simply trust that there is a higher wisdom that knows exactly how to bring about the situation you desire.

Using your imagination means holding a picture in your mind of something you desire. It could be a job opportunity, a wonderful relationship, a beautiful home, or an exciting vacation. The key is to keep your inner focus on the image of what you want to create.

As you use your imagination to picture the outcome you want, feel positive emotions. What would you feel like if you had the situation in your life? Visualize your friends and family being excited for you. See yourself in the scene where you are experiencing this situation you desire. Fill the picture with clear and positive feelings. See yourself being confident and secure. Visualize light and love surrounding you. Feel how excited you are at achieving this goal.

While you are actively engaged in the two steps of imagination and positive emotions, you will find that your inner guidance will begin to give you messages regarding your goals. You'll find that you wake up one morning with an impulse to call someone who is in a position to help you achieve your goal. You may find synchronicities and coincidences beginning to occur. You may also feel a growing confidence or sense of inspiration. Ideas may pop into your head about how to proceed. You may receive a dream that gives you information. Simply be on the lookout for messages from your inner guidance. There is an Intelligent Wisdom that guides the Universe. It provides information through your intuition to help you achieve your goals.

Finally, you need to take action. The key here is not to do something because *you think you should*. Move ahead only when the impulse feels joyful, exciting, and interesting. These impulses are your intuition indicating what action is needed to produce your goal. Your intuition is connected to All-That-Is and knows the most efficient path to get to where you want to go. When you listen to and follow your inner guidance, it will lead you to a life you love.

Intuition Exercise:
The Power of the Pictures in Your Mind

Spend time practicing the steps of the creation process. Write in your journal about your ideal life. Take five minutes every day to visualize and feel yourself achieving your goals. Pay attention to any intuitive guidance that comes your way, and remember to take action only when it feels joyful.

Begin to collect magazines and cut out pictures that represent something you want to create in your life. You might find inspirational words, pictures of exotic places you'd like to visit, a vehicle you'd like to own, a home you'd love to live in, or even images of an ideal relationship you would like to have. I keep my collage over my writing desk and glance at it frequently. Every time I look at it I smile with anticipation, knowing that Divine intelligence is directing its unfolding in my life.

Your Intuition Journal

My clients often tell me that they can clearly state what they *don't* want but find themselves at a loss to describe what they *do* want. It's difficult to begin to create a life you love when you haven't defined what that life might look like! Here are some journal questions to get you started.

What's your goal? What's the outcome you want to create?

What images come to mind as you see yourself achieving your goal?

How will you feel when you achieve your goal?

What is your intuition communicating to you right now about your goal?

Is there any action that you're being guided to take? Is there anything that feels exciting or joyful that you want to act on?

When you're clear about where you're heading, your intuition will begin to give you information about the quickest path to achieving your goals. Pay attention to sudden insights, strong emotions, physical sensations, or mental pictures that may present a clue about the course of action for you to take.

LESSON 33

———◉———

Listen to Your Inner Wisdom

*Intuition is the spontaneous appearance of knowledge:
a new idea, the solution to a problem, a clear sense
of where to go or what to do next. [It occurs] in the
absence of sufficient background or information
to think one's way to that conclusion.*

—Reverend Mary Murray Shelton

One of the questions I'm asked most frequently is, "How do I know it's my intuition and not fear (or ego, wishful thinking, habit of thought)?" I wish I had a simple answer. Wouldn't it be great if the voice of your fear sounded like Darth Vader and the voice of intuition sounded like Celine Dion?! That would be too easy!

One of the best ways to find the answer for yourself is to take a small step toward what you are being prompted to do. How do you feel as you proceed? What are the results you're getting? If you continue to feel positive and your actions produce well-being and harmony, then you're on the right track. Keep going! If, on the other hand, you feel depressed, blocked, and lacking in energy and you're getting a negative response to your actions, it's time to slow down, stop, and reevaluate.

Accurate intuition will inevitably lead you to a place of well-being. The results you achieve will allow you to be of service to others as well as to yourself. When you follow your inner guidance, coincidences and synchronicities begin to occur. Doors will open and opportunities will come your way. You'll find that as you feel your way along the path of following your intuition, more steps will be presented to you.

Sometimes it's a little scary taking those steps, as you don't know exactly where they lead. It's as if you're walking on a path surrounded by fog, and you can see only a few steps in front of you. You have to trust that if you keep putting one foot in front of the other you'll ultimately be led to the place you want to go.

When you have a new goal in your life, ask your intuition for direction. See your task as following any hunch, inspiration, inner voice, or dream you receive. Have faith that your intuition is connected to a greater wisdom in the universe. Affirm that this wisdom knows just the right path for you to follow. As you hold a vision of what you want to create, the wisdom that created the world will assist you in bringing together the perfect set of circumstances to help you grow and flourish.

There is no immediate and correct way of knowing that you're receiving accurate intuition. If you are motivated by the desire to be of service and to do good in the world and you're inspired to take action, take those small steps forward. You'll find that as you continue to listen for guidance and move forward on its wisdom, you'll soon know the answer and doubt will disappear.

Intuition Exercise:
Building Your Intuition Muscles

Learning to trust your intuition is like practicing any new skill or talent. Usually you feel uncertain and insecure. "Am I doing it right?" is often the major question. Here are some simple steps to build your faith in your intuitive guidance as a source of information you can count on to create a life you love.

When you're faced with a decision, find a time and place where you can be still and listen for guidance. Have a pen and paper on hand. Mentally review your concern. You might want to write down a few paragraphs to clarify the issue.

Clear your mind as best you can. Some people do this by watching their breath flow in and out, others by focusing on a candle or listening to relaxing music. Find a way that works best for you.

Ask your inner guidance for information about the best choice. Open-ended questions are most helpful. Here are some examples: "What is the best choice for my work at this time?" "How can I help my daughter?" "How can I increase my prosperity?" "What can I do to improve my health?"

Listen carefully. Don't edit what you receive. Intuition may come in a flash of insight, words, a fleeting or symbolic impression, an emotion, or even a body sensation. Some people report that they suddenly "just know" the answer. Others say the answer comes to them later in the day, when they least expect it.

Write the information in your journal. Evaluate it. If you've received accurate information, it should feel right to you. You will probably experience a pull to action that your guidance created. The information will make you feel peaceful or calm, not agitated or upset.

Take some steps in the direction your intuition indicates. This need not require a huge leap of faith or a big change in your life. Test the information and see what the results are. If you receive positive results and you continue to feel good, take some more steps.

Evaluate your process. Each time you receive accurate information, act on it and create a positive outcome. You're building "intuitive muscle." You're creating a strong channel for Divine wisdom to flow to you easily and effortlessly whenever you need it.

Your Intuition Journal

Practice the above exercise for a few minutes each day. List some issues for which you'd like some Divine insight. Then proceed to ask your intuition these questions, one at a time. It's possible that the information may not make sense to you right now. Write down the guidance you receive. In a few month's time, look back on your notes and reflect on the accuracy of your insights. The answers may make sense from the perspective of hindsight.

LESSON 34

Grow a Prayer Life

*I have not been able to resolve these issues in my life and
I have used every technique I know. I would like to show
my trust in the Divine force by simply turning them over
to your Divine hands. As I do this I know that the Divine
force that is you, God, is also me, and I trust that this
action will lead to a resolution to these problems.*

—Wayne Dyer

What does it mean to "let go and let God"? I remember that when
I first heard that concept—it scared me. It seemed to mean that I
was letting go of all control. I thought that I had to give up any
role in the outcome of my problem. I expected that if I was finally
successful at this surrendering process, God and his angels would
recognize this and immediately swoop in and claim, "She's finally
let it go! Give her what she wants!"

All of us have some challenge in our life that causes us pain or
concern. It may be about the lack of a life partner, a worry about
a health or financial issue, a problem you're experiencing with a
close friend or family member. If it has been in your life for a long
time, you've probably worried, talked, asked for advice from others,

issued ultimatums, and done any number of other things to re-solve the issue. Has it worked? If so, you're allowed to skip to the next chapter!

For the next week try an experiment. For this limited period of time, surrender your concern to God. In effect, you'll be saying to God, "I have struggled and suffered with this problem for too long and I don't know what to do. I am releasing it to you and ask for your intervention and wisdom, so I may experience peace and harmony in my life."

Your job now is to let it go and not worry or agonize. You may find yourself becoming concerned with the issue from time to time. Simply say to yourself, "I've tried everything else and now I'm trusting God." Know that Divine wisdom is flowing through you at all times. Know that there is an abundance of love, help, healing, and wisdom working with you to provide a solution. As you practice this letting-go process, pay attention to any insights, hunches, or changes in attitude that occur. The answer to the prob-lem may not come in the form you expect, but it always comes.

Intuition Exercise: Relax into Love and Light

Relax into peace and close your eyes. Take a deep breath and let it out as you sigh deeply. Imagine the sun glowing brightly above you. (Pause.) It fills you with warmth and light. (Pause.) Allow the light to fill your body and surround you. (Pause.) Imagine that this light connects you with the wisdom of the Universe. (Pause.) Breathe in this wisdom, knowing that as you connect with it in your mind, it is in you and all around you. (Pause.) You have access to this Divine wisdom.

Relax even further into the oneness. Breathe deeply and relax into this light and loving energy. Your only intention for now is simply to experience it and be present. (Pause.) Let go of all thoughts as you bask in the universal flow of love and light.

Continue to experience this light and connection to Divine wisdom for as long as you choose. As you near the end of your meditation, affirm the power of love and light to bring you insight, mental clarity, and physical healing, and to bring the same to each individual you hold in your mind. See this light and feel this light bringing healing to you and all those around you.

If you have an issue or concern, bring it to mind and ask a question. Wait patiently and expectantly. Pay attention to your feelings, body sensations, thoughts, words, and images. Imagine that you are releasing your issue or concerns into the hands of God. You are surrendering your concern, trusting that a resolution will come about in the perfect way and at the perfect time.

As you end your meditation, bring to mind all that you have in your life for which you are grateful. Affirm that you are open to Divine guidance in all forms today and in the days to come. Give thanks.

Your Intuition Journal

Is there some problem that you've been struggling with for months, years, or your whole life? The perennial challenges that many of us face are concerns about relationships, health, money, family, and career. Is there something that often keeps you awake at night? That's the issue to turn over to God.

> What issue have you been struggling with for a long time?
> What does it mean to you to "surrender it to God"?
> Are you willing to ask for help from God?
> If not, what's stopping you?
> What are you willing to do?

If the idea of surrendering this issue to God is one you wish to pursue, try the "letting go" exercise. Whenever you begin to worry or obsess about this concern, say to yourself, "I have let this go to God. A Higher Power is working on resolving this issue to the greatest good of all concerned." As soon as you've said this, immediately take the focus off your worry, release it, and shift your attention to something more pleasant.

LESSON 35

---———◼◗◼———---

Cultivate a Positive Attitude

*We are what we think. All that we are arises with
our thoughts. With our thoughts we make the world.*

—Buddha

We've all had those times in our lives when everything seems to
go wrong. You keep trying to pick yourself back up, yet you keep
falling back down. It's as if everything in your life seems to be conspiring against you. You're worried about money to pay the bills,
your company is threatening a layoff, your car is making strange
(and expensive-sounding) noises, and one of your parents is sick.
You feel like you're barely coming up for air.

Where is your intuition in all this disaster that's facing you? Who
has the time or the inclination to tune in and check out their
inner wisdom during a crisis? It's during these times of overwhelming stress that you most need your inner guidance to steer
your life back to peace and tranquillity. Your intuition is still
there, ready and willing to provide direction, but you may have to
use a different set of skills to access it.

What you say to yourself during extremely stressful periods in
your life can make all the difference. I'm not suggesting sugar-
coated affirmations here. There is nothing worse than affirming,

"I am blissful, content, and serene" when you're anything but. Nor does saying, "I live in an abundant universe and have plenty of money" make sense when you are barely putting food on the table.

Try an experiment for just a moment. Bring to mind a stressful event in your life. Now close your eyes and say the words "I'm so overwhelmed! What can I do?!" several times and with intense feeling. Then, with the same event in mind, say the words "I'm open to new possibilities" or "I know I'll be shown the best way out of this situation." How do you feel? Do you notice that the first sentence makes you feel shut down and anxious? The second and third statements probably made you feel open and hopeful and produced an expectation of positive change.

Your intuition is always there to guide you. It doesn't leave you in the lurch when you most need it. It hasn't disappeared from your life as soon as a crisis hits. I know that it frequently feels that way. We often speak of intuition as a "still, quiet inner voice." I wish there was a switch to turn up the volume on that quiet wisdom during times of crisis. We have such a cacophony of other inner voices vying for attention. The voices we usually hear the loudest are the ones that say, "I'm scared. I'm overwhelmed. I'm alone. Get me out of this mess!" Try the following exercise when you need to get through a difficult period.

Intuition Exercise:
Calm Words During Times of Stress

Here are some words to use to help you feel calm and open you to the guidance you need during times of stress. Feel free to mix and match any of them. Some of them may work for you, and others won't. Use the statements that make you feel better and repeat them throughout the day. You'll find that if you do, you'll be more receptive to hearing direction from Divine Intuition and be more able to act on its wisdom to guide you to a peaceful resolution to the conflict you're experiencing.

"I know that I'll feel better soon."

"Healing is taking place within me."

"I am safe, surrounded and protected by a loving wisdom."

"I trust myself to get through this situation. I know I'm strong."

"Support is coming from a variety of sources. I am open to receive all loving assistance."

"I know that new doors to opportunity will open as I go through this transition."

"I know that I have to let go of the old in order for the new to be born."

"I deserve a life that is balanced, abundant, and full of rich possibilities."

"I am open and receptive to new avenues of abundance."

"I am guided through this day. I know that I will make the right choices."

"Good will come out of this situation. I need to be patient as it unfolds."

"I have control over my thoughts, and right now I am choosing to feel peace, not fear."

"My life is unfolding in new ways. Things will get better."

"I'm willing to let go of people and situations that drain me. I create space for love and kindness in my life."

"I know that the future contains wonderful opportunities for me to flourish and grow."

You may want to consider putting the statements on Post-it notes in locations where you'll see them often. For example, place them on the wall above your desk, on a mirror, in your wallet, by your bed, or on your refrigerator.

Your Intuition Journal

Commit to writing a few sentences in your journal each day. It may be the last thing you feel like doing during a stressful period, but it's often the most helpful. Writing can get you out of your standard approaches and help you see things from a fresh perspective.

Which of the statements in the Intuition Exercise did you resonate with the most? Write them in your journal.

What good or positive things happened today that reflected the truth of the above statement?

What guidance did you receive today that you feel good about taking action on?

LESSON 36

—◉—

The Divine Connection Is Always On

Remember that whatever you want to know or
accomplish in your life is possible if you are truly ready
to trust in your Divine powers to manifest it. You will
find that the appropriate teachers will appear for you,
and that you will be guided in the right direction.

—Wayne Dyer

I got up early this morning to begin writing this chapter on creating a Divine connection. I felt stuck. What can I say that's relevant? I began doing the diversionary stuff that all writers are familiar with. I listened to my voice mail. I got myself another cup of coffee. Ate a peach and scanned a couple of other books on the topic. I called a friend to say hi. I sat at my desk again. Hmmm . . . what to write? Ah! The ultimate diversion—check my e-mail! I was successfully signed on for all of three seconds when a message flashed on the screen: YOU HAVE BEEN DISCONNECTED. Hah! Wouldn't it be great if our guidance was always so quick, accurate, and to the point?!

The message I'd just received was that I wasn't checking in with my own inner guidance for assistance in writing this chapter. I was allowing myself to be distracted by everything and everyone around me. How often do you do that in your daily life? You might be searching the Help Wanted section of your local paper looking for a job, or desperately trying to find a new place to live because your lease is about to end, or trying to figure out how to cope with a coworker who's making your job an ordeal. You can certainly choose to tackle this all on your own, or you can remember to check in with the Universe and ask for help and guidance. You are not alone; help is always at hand.

We all know how important prayer and meditation are. Hopefully, you take at least a few moments every day to consciously commune with God, ask for guidance and insight, and rest in the abundance of love that surrounds and fills you. But what about your life between prayers? What do you do when you're full of doubt and fear and are continually questioning whether you have chosen the right path? Do you need to be in a constant state of prayer to have a successful life? In a word, yes.

I don't mean the kind of prayer where you're on your knees beseeching God to grant your desires, nor do I mean to imply that you should sit in a yoga position for hours on end communing with Spirit. Saint Teresa of Avila wrote, "For prayer is nothing else than being on terms of friendship with God." When you are in touch with your Divine Intuition you have an open channel through which pours love, reassurance, inspiration, new ideas, and direction.

The Universe communicates with us in so many ways. Your job is to keep the lines of transmission open by checking in with your inner guidance whenever you have a doubt, question, or concern. In the film *Star Wars*, Obi-Wan Kenobi tells Luke Skywalker, "The Force is an energy field created by all living things. It surrounds us, it penetrates us, it binds galaxies together." He adds that the way to connect with the Force is to "follow your feelings." He's speaking of one of the ways we access Divine wisdom.

The answers are always there, ready for the taking. God is not something that can be turned on or off. The love and wisdom that are God are everywhere, all the time. Just ask for direction and the answers will begin to flow. You stand always in a Universe full of abundance and love. Choose to embrace it and your life will begin to unfold in miraculous ways. May the Force be with you.

Intuition Exercise:
Making the Connection with the Divine

Following are some ways to connect with your Divine Intuition when you're in the midst of a busy day, and time and circumstances aren't conducive to a lengthy meditation.

Ask yourself, "What would ——— do?" Fill in the blank with the name of someone you admire: Jesus, Buddha, Oprah, or your Aunt Pat. It can be anyone who represents inner strength and wisdom to you.

Look toward heaven and send a silent prayer to God, in essence saying, "Help me out here. I need your presence and desire connection with you."

Close your eyes for just a moment and visualize the outcome you desire. As you rehearse it in your mind, you're apt to receive information from your intuition as to how you can achieve your goal.

Feel your connection with the Universe in whatever way works for you and silently affirm, "I'm okay. God and I can handle this."

Author and minister Mary Manin Morrissey makes her connection with Spirit this way: "God, help me remember to turn to You for the strength I need, instead of trying to do everything on my own. Let me be willing to receive Your help through both the still, small voice of insight and the assistance of others."

Find a quiet place—a bathroom, your car, or an empty office—and simply close your eyes and imagine inhaling love and peace. Feel your connection to the Divine. Imagine angels wrapping their wings around you to comfort, protect, and guide you.

Often when we get caught up in fear and anxiety it's because we're dwelling on something that hasn't happened. "Will the bills get paid?" "Will I get laid off?" Take a few minutes to look around you and focus on the present moment. Fill your thoughts with everything you have in your life that you feel grateful for.

Placing your palms together as if in prayer is a very centering experience. It's a common gesture and doesn't usually get unduly noticed by anyone else. When I'm feeling stressed or anxious I do this symbolic gesture to remind myself to stay calm and connect to Spirit.

My friend Laura suggested this technique. She had a student in a class who was being angry and disruptive. She took a deep breath, feeling her connection with God. As she exhaled, she looked directly at the angry student and imagined that all the love, compassion, and healing she felt was being sent to and received by him. Things immediately calmed down, and she was able to use the incident as a teaching point.

Most people at work take a coffee break. You can take a Spirit break. Take a few moments to go for a walk with the intention of connecting with the Universe in whatever way feels right to you. Simply getting out of the building and taking a few deep breaths of air or feeling the sun on your skin may be enough for you to remember your Spirit through the rest of the day.

Your Intuition Journal

The worst time to create a strategy for stress reduction is when you're already under stress! As you write in your journal, think about some of your own ideas that will help you *maintain* a more peaceful and balanced life.

Look at the suggestions listed in the intuition exercise above. Which one or two do you feel would be most helpful to you in your life?

List three things that cause you stress on a daily basis.

What are some ways for you to connect with the Universe in order to feel calmer and less stressed about these issues?

LESSON 37

───◈───

From Crisis to Opportunity

When one door of happiness closes, another opens;
but often we look so long at the closed door that we
do not see the one that has been opened for us.

—Helen Keller

Many people have told me heartbreaking tales about injuries, illnesses, accidents, and near disasters. They often follow their story by saying something like "I should have listened to my intuition." Has this happened to you? Have you ignored a message from your intuition, or are you ignoring one now?

There is usually a pattern to intuitive messages before a full-blown crisis erupts.

You're uncomfortable about something. This could be a physical discomfort or simply a feeling that something is wrong.

Your intuition tells you to slow down, speak up, or make a change of some sort. You ignore these messages.

Your situation gets worse. You feel a cold coming on, get into a minor accident, or find yourself arguing with others more than usual. You feel tense and uptight. You're not sleeping well.

Your inner messages indicate that it's time for a significant change. You need to reevaluate some aspect of your life because it is causing you major discomfort. This is a time to take a few days off, get away, write in your journal, meditate, go for walks, listen to your dreams, talk to friends or a therapist.

You continue to ignore the messages. A crisis erupts. You get into a major accident. You're given notice at work. You discover that your spouse is having an affair. Your doctor informs you that you're at risk for a major illness. Your life is headed for a major disaster.

Analysis: your intuition has been trying to restore balance and equilibrium to your life. It's been telling you quietly but insistently, "Time for a change . . . NOW!" By ignoring the messages you received, you put yourself on a path where sooner or later you'd be *forced* to make a change.

Here's how this scenario played out with my client Beth. She told me her tale of getting sideswiped in the high-speed lane on an interstate highway. Her car was totaled, and she was taken by ambulance to the hospital with major neck and back injuries, as well as a broken arm. When I saw her she still had a cast on her arm and she was wearing a neck brace. Beth's first words were, "I knew something like this would happen."

She reported that her life had felt increasingly stressful. She hated her job. She had a boss who was placing unreasonable demands on her, requiring that she stay late, work on weekends, and meet unrealistic deadlines for projects. "I knew that there was no way to please him, and yet the more unreasonable he got, the more stubborn I became. I was going to extraordinary lengths to prove to him that I was good at my work. Every part of me was screaming that it was time to look for another job. I felt like I was in a pressure cooker. The accident didn't surprise me because I was so stressed and felt I had no options. The accident gave me a way out of my situation." She began to cry. "I just wish I had listened to my intuition. I wouldn't have had to go through these months of pain if I'd acted on what I already knew."

The key to avoiding disasters is to catch the "messages" when they first show up. Intuition doesn't hold up a big sign saying, "Disaster About to Occur. Slow Down Now." These warning signs are often not much louder than a whisper. It's the proverbial "still, quiet voice" that says, "You need to spend time with your spouse and children." Or "You're putting everyone else first and not taking time for yourself." Or "You wake up each day hating your job. You need to look for something else that inspires you." You may rationalize that you "don't have time." Yet when you don't make the time, crises begin to occur.

Beth called last week to say that she had found a new job with a wonderful boss. She enjoys going to work every day. She reported, "I'll never ignore those inner messages again. I could have made it so much easier!"

Intuition Exercise:
Learning to Heed the Warning Signs

1. Getting the message. Has there ever been a little voice in your head that kept saying, "You've got to slow down," "You need to rest," "You're working too hard," or "You need to take care of this now"? Did you choose to ignore the voice? Did you miss the message? I have found that if we're honest with ourselves, we'll admit there was an intuitive message we ignored before a crisis. Take a moment and think about a crisis that occurred in your life. It could be a relationship that ended, an accident you had, a job you lost, or a serious illness you contracted.

2. Intuition warnings. Intuition usually gives us messages in a number of ways. Did you have uncomfortable physical sensations, such as tension in your shoulders, a chronically upset stomach, or headaches that you ignored?

Did you find yourself consistently experiencing strong emotions, such as anger, jealousy, rage, or fear? Powerful, negative emotions are an important indicator that something is significantly out of balance in your life and needs to be addressed.

Did you receive "warnings" in your dreams? If your intuition can't seem to get through to you during your normal waking hours, it may try to get your attention during your sleep. If your dream state suddenly changes from serene to anxious or violent, it might be helpful to pay attention. Dreams that show you're feeling out of control, such as not being able to use the brakes in your car or images of not being able to move, could be a message from your intuition. These nightmares might indicate a need for you to take control, stand up for yourself or shift your attitude about a stressful situation in your waking life.

3. Heeding the message. Do you remember receiving any or all of these warning signs? What would you do differently next time?

Your Intuition Journal

How often have you said, "I should have listened to my intuition" or "I knew something bad was going to happen"? You may know exactly what you should be doing, but you don't slow down enough to listen to your inner voice or come up with a strategy to change the situation. Here's your chance to stop, look, listen, and respond!

Write down any messages you're receiving right now in the following areas.

Relationship
Work/career
Spirituality
Family
Health
Friends
Goals
Social life
Fun/play/enjoyment
Other

In which areas are you receiving the strongest messages?
What action(s) are you willing to take to improve these situations?

LESSON 38

Dream Power

Dreams are my compass and my truth;
they guide me and link me to the divine.

—Judith Orloff

Many people find that their dreams are a gateway for intuitive wisdom. Dreams can help us make decisions, resolve conflicts, explore new behaviors, and create new options. Since ancient times, dreams have been used to find answers to our deepest questions.

Dreams speak to us in symbolic images, which is one of the primary ways intuition communicates. By paying attention to your dreams, you can receive insight, empowerment, and clear direction about your life goals. You spend about a third of your life asleep, so why not use that time to your advantage?

Experts differ widely on interpreting the symbolism of dreams. One group prefers to believe that there is only one absolute meaning for each dream symbol. Another group embraces the idea that dream interpretations can vary from one individual to another. Thus one person dreaming about a fire might see it as a warning of danger. Another person having a similar dream might feel that the fire indicates warmth and romance.

I belong in the latter camp. I believe that your dreams provide you with valuable wisdom from your soul, and that you are the ultimate authority on what those messages mean. Dr. Brugh Joy, author of the book *Joy's Way* and an expert on dreaming as a transformational tool, states, "The best dream analysts are intuitive." He claims that when you hit on the correct interpretation of a dream, you feel a "zing," a sensation that you're in tune with what the dream was communicating.

All dream researchers agree on one thing: if you want to gain valuable insight from your dreams, you need a system for remembering them and writing them down. Have you ever had a dream that was so vivid and intense that it woke you up out of a sound sleep? At the time, you probably said to yourself that you had no need to write it down because you knew you wouldn't forget it. Yet, by morning, the dream had lapsed into a foggy, distant memory of *something*, but you couldn't remember what.

Many wonderful books have been written on dreams and dream interpretation. Please seek them out and study this issue if you find that dreams are an especially helpful way for you to receive intuitive guidance.

Intuition Exercise:
Divining Wisdom from Your Dreams

Following is a simple overview of how to gain inner wisdom from your dreams.

Before going to bed, write a few sentences about something you are concerned about.

Summarize the issue into a question and write it in your journal. Keep it short, simple, and direct. You can ask open-ended questions such as, "What shall I do now regarding this issue?" or "What is my best choice?" Or if you're trying to decide between two courses of action, ask about only one alternative: "Should I choose option A?" not "Should I choose A or B?"

Repeat your question in your mind as you drift off to sleep. Visualize yourself awakening with the answer. Some people find it helpful to also repeat an affirmation such as "I remember my dreams and they provide wise guidance."

Write down your dreams, or at least a few notes about them, the moment you wake up.

The answer to your previous night's question may be immediately apparent to you upon writing down your dream. If not, don't despair! Many times the answer to your question may pop into your mind later in the day, when you least expect it. You can also try repeating the exercise over the next few nights and see if an answer emerges over time.

Trust the process. Be observant for those "zings" of insight. Learning to use and interpret dreams is a skill like any other. The good news is that you get to learn while you sleep. How many talents can you say that about?!

Your Intuition Journal

As you begin to work with your dreams, you'll find that certain dream symbols appear again and again. Use your journal to write down the symbols that seem to be the most powerful, evoke the strongest feelings, or keep reappearing in your dreams. Then take time to explore their deeper meanings.

A simple technique is to create a dream-symbol chart. For each recurring symbol answer the following questions:

1. What feeling do you associate with the symbol?

2. When you visualize the image, what immediately pops into your mind?

3. Is there a pun that could be associated with this image? (For example; sun = son; coin = change)

4. Imagine yourself being the actual symbol and speaking in the first person. For example, if you have a dream that involves

a bird in a cage, the bird might say, "I feel trapped and confined. I want to break free and fly." This may provide some insight about the meaning of the image.

5. What is your best understanding of what this symbol represents?

LESSON 39

———◦❉◦———

How to Work with Indecision

Once you make a decision, the universe
conspires to make it happen.

—Ralph Waldo Emerson

It can feel like hell on earth when you're in the grip of indecision. You wake up in the morning certain you have made the right decision, only to change your mind after you've had your first sip of coffee. "Will my relationship get better or should I just leave now and cut my losses?" "Should I take that job or will opportunities open up in the one I have?" These are the kinds of questions that can keep you awake at two A.M. and plague your daytime hours with feelings of massive anxiety.

At the core of any decision, you want a guarantee that things will work out. You want to know the future and have an iron-clad pledge from the Universe that you will be happier, healthier, and more successful if you make the right choice. It's tempting to just "not decide" and let fate take its course. However, not deciding is in itself a decision, and you owe it to yourself to make a positive choice in order to create a life you love.

What role does intuition play in this endless game of Should I, Shouldn't I? A big one! As the Intuition Exercise in this chapter explains, when you pay attention to your intuition, it will provide you with step-by-step guidance to make these important decisions.

Does it take courage to make these changes? Yes! Courage is doing what you're afraid to do, and everyone experiences it before they take a risk. Does it take more than a little faith? Yes! You're taking an action to create something better, and it helps to have faith in yourself, as well as faith in a Higher Power that will provide assistance. You may have to "Leap [and know] the net will appear!" as writer Julia Cameron puts it.

Many people wait to decide until everything is perfect. It never is! There will always be difficulties, challenges, and obstacles. What I've discovered is that with each step you take, the Universe expands your options. Doors that you thought were closed will begin to open. When you make a decision, you take a stand. You are telling the Universe what you want, and as Emerson said, "the universe conspires to make it happen."

Intuition Exercise:
Getting to Good Decisions

There are many ways to receive intuitive guidance when making a decision. No one way is the right way. Your success will come as you understand and develop the right way for you.

Write several sentences about a decision you're facing.

For the purpose of this exercise, give yourself two options. Write them down this way:

Choice A:

Choice B:

Imagine yourself making the decision to go with Choice A. Close your eyes and ask yourself the following questions. Then repeat the exercise with Choice B.

How do I feel about this decision?

Good decision: You feel elated and enthusiastic.

Bad decision: You feel down and depressed.

How do I experience this decision in my body?

Good decision: You experience lightness, openness, or flexibility.

Bad decision: Your stomach or shoulders tighten at the thought of pursuing this choice.

Do any words pop into your mind when you think of this option?

Good decision: You hear words like "Yes!" or "Go for it!"

Bad decision: You hear words like "No!" or "This won't work."

Do you receive any visual impressions when thinking about this choice?

Good decision: Positive or optimistic images surround the symbolic representation of this decision.

Bad decision: You see an X through the decision, or you see some other negative image.

After you've gone through this exercise, what choice does your intuition indicate?

Your Intuition Journal

Do you hate to make decisions? Perhaps you fear making a mistake, moving out of your comfort zone, or changing your life in some irreparable way. Or you might have a decision-making style similar to that of Marilyn Monroe, who said, "Ever notice that 'what the hell' is always the right decision?" If you'd like to create a better plan, write the answers to the following questions in your journal.

Think back to a time when you made a major decision. Describe it here.

In retrospect, was it a good decision or a bad decision?

Did you listen to or ignore your intuition as you were making this decision?

Was the outcome what you'd hoped for?

What do you wish you had done differently?

What part of your decision-making process worked well for you?

In reviewing what you just wrote, what have you learned that you can apply to your current decision?

LESSON 40

The Courage to Persevere

*There are people who put their dreams in a little box and
say, "Yes, I've got dreams, of course I've got dreams."
Then they put the box away and bring it out once in a
while to look in it, and yep, they're still there. These are
great dreams, but they never even get out of the box.
It takes an uncommon amount of guts to put your
dreams on the line. . . . That's where courage comes in.*

—Erma Bombeck

Have you ever yearned for something, taken some courageous steps
toward achieving it, and failed in your efforts? I met with a rather
depressed young women recently. She spoke about her hopes and
dreams in the past tense. "I tried to be an actress and it didn't
work." "I wanted to start my own business and I didn't have any
luck." "I had hoped to get married but there were no good guys left
out there." At age twenty-six she had put her dreams in a box and
given up on life. Perseverance and courage are important tools
when following your intuition.

It's your intuition speaking when you feel bored, depressed, and
enervated. The message is "Change is needed!" It's your intuition
speaking when you feel excited or even mildly interested in something. The message is "Take steps to follow that dream!" What is

the message when you've tried and failed? "Pick yourself up, dust yourself off, continue to check in with your intuition, and adjust your course." A bend in the road is not the end of the road unless you fail to make the turn.

All of us want to succeed. No one wants to fail. However, most of the people who have seemingly achieved overnight success took a long time getting there! They had to adjust their course many times. Joey Green writes in his book *The Road to Success Is Paved with Failure* that:

> Rosie O'Donnell dropped out of Boston College after her drama professor told her that she would never make it as an actress.
>
> Jay Leno applied for work at Woolworth's but failed the employment test.
>
> Marilyn Monroe was fired by Twentieth Century–Fox because production chief Darryl Zanuck considered her unattractive.
>
> Thomas Edison was fired from his job working in a telegraph office after one of his chemical experiments exploded.
>
> Orville Wright was expelled from the sixth grade for "mischievous behavior."
>
> Walt Disney's first cartoon-production company went bankrupt.
>
> Jerry Seinfeld sold light bulbs over the telephone.
>
> Madonna peddled doughnuts at a Times Square shop.
>
> John F. Kennedy lost the election for president of his freshman class at Harvard.
>
> John Grisham's first novel, *A Time to Kill*, was rejected by sixteen agents and a dozen publishing houses.

It's dreadful to fail. However, the danger in failing is not the actual act of failure. It's what you tell yourself about your seeming defeat. Close your eyes and say to yourself, "It's over. I'll never be a success. Nothing works for me." How do you feel? Pretty desperate and hopeless, right? But failure itself is merely a statement saying,

"This way doesn't work." That's why your immediate reaction is so important! Now close your eyes and say to yourself, "I still believe in myself and my dreams. I trust my inner guidance to show me a new direction that points the way to success." Feels better, right? (You'll have to find the words that feel best for you.) In the second option, you open yourself up to guidance, hope, new ideas, and possibilities.

Everyone has a dream or objective in life. Think about your dreams right now. Is there something you're not going for because you're scared you won't succeed? Most of your battle is right between your ears. It's often been said that we have nothing to fear but fear itself. When you give in to fear and stop trying, you suffer the ultimate consequence—no success!

In my work as an intuition coach, I often urge people to set goals that encourage them to stretch their comfort zone. I ask them to forget what they think they "should" do and design goals that make them feel good. I also ask them to break their goals down into three-month, six-month, one-year, and five-year plans. If you haven't achieved your stated goals during the time period, change your approach. Instead of thinking, "I haven't met my financial goals this year. What a failure!" shift your focus and ask your intuition for guidance. "What do I need to do now in order to achieve my goal?" Be kind and gentle with yourself. You don't have to stay in a stuck place or beat yourself up with endless recriminations. Where does that get you? Most of the time you can pick yourself up, make some adjustments, and be on your way.

When I'm working with my clients I often hear my own inner voice whispering, "Tell them to have courage and to try again." Your past does not equal your future. Yesterday's failure does not predict your future outcomes. You're a different person than you were five years ago. Nothing is a failure if you learn something from the experience. Things don't go always go the way you'd planned. It might be helpful to think about these temporary set-backs as God's way of helping you to grow "strong in the broken places," as Ernest Hemingway said.

Intuition Exercise:
Moving Toward Success

Here's a plan to accomplish your goals while you work in harmony with your intuition.

Focus on the goal. When you think of an ideal day, week, month, or year, what are you doing with your life?

Develop a plan. What are the small steps you can begin to take that will lead you in the direction you want to go? Lao-tzu said, "A journey of a thousand miles begins with the first step." Take that first step, and then take another.

If you get off track, be willing to change. What are you doing that's on the mark? If one way doesn't work for you, be ready to go another. Many times, the road to success is found by taking a detour.

Cultivate the attitude of a wish fulfilled. Success is waiting for you—feel it, see it, vividly imagine it, sense it, and grasp it.

Don't dwell on the old. Put your mental energy and action into focusing on where you want to go.

Look ahead, rather than back. Ask yourself, "How will I view this circumstance six months or a year from now?" Put your focus on what you have the power to change rather than dwelling on an apparent failure.

How will you know when you're succeeding? Success isn't a destination; it's a journey. Here's a checklist:

> Are you enjoying what you do?
> Are your connections with friends, colleagues, and family strengthened by your success?

Are you proud of your accomplishments thus far?

In the process of achieving your goals, are you developing the qualities of kindness, self-respect, courage, compassion, patience, love, and hope?

Do you feel more in control of yourself and your life?

Are you able to shift negative self-talk to something more positive and useful?

Has your spiritual life been enriched through the process of achieving this goal?

Are you being of service to others?

Are you more self-confident and sure of your capabilities as the result of pursuing this dream?

Are you continuing to stretch just beyond your comfort zone?

Are you easily able to shift direction if the course you've been on isn't working?

Are you consistently listening to your inner guidance and following its wisdom?

If you answered yes to most or all of these questions, you are a success!

Your Intuition Journal

When you've put a lot of hard work into an endeavor and it's not going as you planned, it's hard to step back and assess the situation. Is there something that you feel you're "failing" at in your life? The following questions will help you put some perspective on your experience.

What can you learn from this?

What are you doing right?

What outcome will make you feel you're successful?

Where did this begin to go wrong?

What do you wish you had done differently?

What is your intuition telling you to do about this situation?

After answering the above questions, do you feel there's a different way to approach your project or endeavor? Depending on the issue, you have several options. You could:

Quit.
Persevere.
Alter your course.
Put the project on hold for a period of time.
Try something new.
Ask for advice from someone who has been successful in a similar endeavor.
Work on your project part-time.
Discuss the situation with others who may be involved.

Which of these options feels best to you? You can choose more than one, and your intuition may present you with even more choices than are listed here. Trust your gut!

LESSON 41

—◦◉◦—

Step Out in Faith

Take the first step in faith. You don't have to
see the whole staircase, just take the first step.

—Dr. Martin Luther King Jr.

One of the biggest challenges facing many of my clients is that they talk themselves out of their hopes and dreams before they even begin. They do this because they can't figure out how to get to where they want to go. I'd like to propose a radical alternative. Don't try to figure out how to reach your goal; let the Universe help you.

Here's my theory: when you hold a strong desire or goal, you send out a vibrational energy that the Universe wants to match. In other words, it wants to help you meet your goal. Your job is to be clear about what you want, to keep your focus off what you don't want, and to take small steps each day based on what you feel excited about. That excitement is your intuition communicating with you. Visualize, affirm, feel, and imagine your successful outcome.

The Universe knows how to make your dream happen. Think of it as a kind of Divine intelligence that has the necessary skills to bring together the exact set of circumstances you need to make your goals a reality. All the logic and intelligence you can muster may not be able to pave the way to this ultimate goal of yours as easily as the Universe can. Let Divine intelligence do its job and orchestrate all the synchronicities, coincidences, and circumstances that need to occur for you to create a life you love.

In my book *Divine Intuition*, I told the story of how my psychic-reading business began. Here's the abbreviated version:

I was the operations manager of a small software company. I hated being there and dreamed of developing my own business. I had taken classes on developing psychic abilities and had found I had a great deal of natural talent in this area. My main concern was "How do I develop a psychic-reading business?!" I quipped that if God posted a "Psychic Reader Wanted" ad in the *Boston Sunday Globe* employment section, I'd apply. Barring that, I wasn't sure where to begin. I decided to practice my newfound consciousness tools of affirming, visualizing, and asking the Universe for help.

About a month into this manifesting process, a friend who had been sick for a long time died. As I walked into the room for his funeral service I felt a strong intuitive inclination to sit next to a woman I hadn't met before. I briefly questioned my reasons for sitting there, as there were quite a few people in the room whom I both knew and preferred to sit next to for emotional support.

At the end of the service the woman and I started talking, and she asked me what I did for a living. Have you ever had one of those times when your brain doesn't engage with your mouth? Despite the fact that in my current job I was an operations manager, I answered, "I'm a psychic." I was immediately stricken with alarm. Why had I answered this way? What would she think?! Yes, I had done readings for a few friends, and friends of friends, but never had I defined my career that way! I felt flustered by my answer. To my surprise, she was quite open and receptive. She then told me that she was a writer for the *Boston Globe* and would love to have a reading so she could write about it in her column.

To make a long story short: she wrote the article, and over the next several months some four hundred people called me to schedule an appointment. Here is the moral of the story from my perspective:

the Universe had managed to create a full-time psychic-reading business virtually overnight. There was no way that I could have created that if I had taken a step-by-step logical approach. Over the past twenty-five years I have seen this process occur over and over again in my life and the lives of my clients. I believe there is a Divine intelligence that works with each and every one of you to help you create a life you love. In the Intuition Exercise that follows, you'll learn the steps to take to help the Universe help you!

Intuition Exercise: What Do You Really Want?

I'm going to ask you to try some things on pure faith. Try to put aside your natural inclination to make logical sense of this process. Here are the concepts:

There is a Divine intelligence that wants you to succeed. It wants you to be happy about your life and living. It wants you to do the thing or things you're passionate about. That's part of your mission here on earth. It doesn't matter what that mission is, whether it's being a good mother or father, a great dancer, a whiz at accounting, an awe-inspiring athlete, or a profound philosopher. This intelligence wants you to succeed and will do whatever it can to assist you.

Take time each day to visualize and affirm your goal. In this way you add power to the vibrational energy that will attract your goal. Your feelings and emotions are an important part of this process. What does it feel like to have what you want? Use the power of your emotions as you visualize.

You will need to work diligently at keeping your focus off what you don't want and maintain focus on your goal. Learn to redirect your thoughts. When you notice yourself dwelling on pessimistic or negative thoughts, shift your focus to what you want.

Each day take at least one step toward what you're excited about. This might mean signing up for a class, going to an informational interview, joining a club or association, writing an article, making a call, or sending an e-mail. Your excitement is a message from your intuition about the next step to take. Whatever it is—do it!

Your goal should be to enjoy this process. Learn to be grateful for all that you've created. As you move toward your desired outcome, you'll find new objectives emerging. That's fine and as it should be. Remember to have fun!

Your Intuition Journal

Following your intuition does not have to be a time-consuming process. Before you get out of bed each morning, take one to two minutes to answer the following questions:

What do you want to do today that feels enjoyable and will move you toward your goal?

What new ideas about your goal have popped into your mind since yesterday?

What action steps are you willing to take today?

What thoughts or ideas have come to you after practicing your affirmations and visualizations?

Many people find that they awaken with fresh thoughts and ideas. (For others it may be after a large mug of coffee!) If morning is a period of clarity for you, take advantage of that by paying attention to any intuitive information that comes to you during that time. If you're a night person, try a meditation before going to bed at night and ask for some Divine insight.

LESSON 42

———◦◉◦———

The Purpose of Your Life

I discovered that people are not really afraid of dying;
they're afraid of not ever having lived, not ever having
deeply considered their life's higher purpose, and not
ever having stepped into that purpose and at least
tried to make a difference in this world.

—Joseph Jaworski

You come to this life on earth with specific talents and intentions. Through your inner guidance you begin to understand and use these gifts. You come here with an assignment, or a life purpose, if you will. It may be the task of raising a family, transforming a business, communicating your ideas as a teacher, or being a leader in your community. Your task may be a massive one, such as raising the level of constructive communication between warring countries, or awakening a consciousness of love and forgiveness in a segment of the population. Whatever purpose your soul has come to unfold, through your Divine Intuition you are given guidance and life experiences that will prepare you to fulfill it.

Many people assume that this life purpose is a job or career they are here to fulfill. Sometimes our purpose is not a *thing* we need to do but a quality we need to develop in order for our soul to unfold and grow to the next level. Through a physical disability you might learn to let others help you or, conversely, learn self-reliance. You may have grown up in an abusive home and learned about empathy and forgiveness. In many sessions with clients I sense a quality that they are here to develop, such as resiliency, patience, or courage.

Following are some other common life lessons. This is meant to be not a comprehensive list of life purposes but, rather, an overview of possibilities. As you read these, see if any particularly resonate with you. The purpose of your life may be to:

Heal a relationship with another individual or group of individuals.

Develop a specific characteristic, such as love, forgiveness, hope, compassion, patience, courage, or faith.

Invent a service or product that will help and assist humankind.

Create works of art and beauty to help heal the souls of others.

Open your heart after an experience of loss and be a model for helping others do the same.

Display courage, integrity, or honesty during a personal or professional difficulty.

Foster open and nonjudgmental communication within a family, neighborhood, or office, or in the world at large.

Aid in the spiritual development of others.

Create a strong family in order to foster the life purpose of yourself, your spouse, and your children.

Release a focus on fear, worry, and anxiety and transform it with the qualities of love, patience, and faith.

When you know your life purpose, you tap into a source of power that enables you to achieve your goals more easily and effectively. Susan Jeffers, the author of *Feel the Fear and Do It Anyway*, wrote, "We become powerful in the face of our fears when we have a sense that we make a difference in this world." As your purpose in life evolves, you'll find yourself with more clarity, energy, and abundance.

Intuition Exercise:
Discovering Your Life Purpose

If you don't yet know your life purpose, here's an exercise for you.

What are three of your best qualities? (For example: I am a loyal friend. I'm patient, kind, and inspiring to others.)

What are some areas of your life where you have difficulty. (For example: I have a tough time telling others how I feel. I'm not very patient. I'm extremely afraid of risk.)

Write about all the things you love to do and then write about why you like to do them. (For example: I love to study healing because I feel that I can contribute to making others feel better. I love to cook because I enjoy entertaining my friends and providing healthy meals for my family. I enjoy writing because I can get my message out to a lot of people.)

What are some qualities you'd like to develop? (Examples: I'd like to be more extroverted. I'd like to laugh more and be less serious. I'd like to be a kinder person.)

After completing the questions above, fill in the blanks to the following sentences. Take whatever answer pops into your mind. Don't *think* about it too much; let your intuition be your guide.

In this life, I have come here to learn _____.

I am also here to develop my _____.

The gifts (positive qualities and characteristics) I have brought with me are _____

and _____

and my ability to _____.

I believe that my life purpose is _____

and _____.

Having completed the exercise, what are some ways you could use this information? Perhaps the insights will help you develop a specific quality, renew your passion for a cause, or simply have more courage as you face a challenging time in your life.

Your Intuition Journal

Many books have been written on the topic of "life purpose." My hope is that this chapter will at least provide some food for thought. Here are some further questions to ponder for your journal entry:

What did you discover about yourself after completing the above lesson and exercise?

What do you think you might need to work on more?

What new skills would you like to learn to enhance your life purpose?

What have you been passionate about in your life?

What would you like to change in the world?

Remember that your life purpose need not be a huge project or undertaking. It may be a quality you develop or a gift you share with your immediate family and community. Listen to the still, small voice within and allow it to show you your purpose.

LESSON 43

———◆◎◆———

Change Your Beliefs
and Change Your Life

*What we see in the outer is but a reflection of the inner,
because we surround ourselves with a picture of our own
beliefs. In other words, we manifest in general what we
seriously think and believe. So if we want to find out
what our habitual thinking is like, we have but to look
around us and ask ourselves what we really see.*

—Emmet Fox

When I began my business many years ago, I gave my clients fairly
traditional "psychic readings." I talked to them about what I saw
in their future. A traditional reading implies the philosophy that
the future is etched in stone and you cannot change it. Your fate
is sealed by some unknown force—God, karma, or kismet. Over a
period of several years, I began to doubt that assumption. I began
to read people's beliefs.

I came to understand that what my clients held in their minds,
or what they believed, created what occurred in their lives. The
beliefs they held created their future. This presented a huge
dilemma for me. I could no longer simply tell clients, "Here's what

I see for you." I began to talk to them about how they create their lives and the events that happen to them.

Discovering and correcting limiting beliefs is absolutely essential if you want to create a life you love. Here are some examples of limiting beliefs:

Life is difficult and suffering is unavoidable.
I'll never get ahead.
I was born unlucky.
All good things must come to an end.
If something good happens, something bad must follow.
You have to work hard every day in order to succeed.
This is my lot in life. You can't change things.
Money doesn't come easily.
The rich get richer. The poor get poorer.
When you get old, you inevitably get sick, weak, and feeble.
There's not enough to go around.
I did something bad in a past life and I'm paying for it
in this life.

Many people have individual beliefs that impair their ability to create a life they love. Here are some examples I call the tyranny of "not enoughs": I'm not smart enough. I'm not educated enough. I'm not thin enough. I'm not old (or young) enough. I'm not rich enough.

Just writing down all those limitations makes me depressed! The main point is that if any one of those limiting beliefs is true for you, you'll have trouble creating a life you love. That's why simple affirmations don't always work. If you repeat the affirmation "I am healthy" and yet you firmly believe that as you grow older you inevitably become chronically ill and weak, you have a strong opposing core belief and your affirmations will probably be ineffective.

You may receive wise guidance every moment of the day, but if you have strongly held negative beliefs, this guidance won't be able to get through. You won't let in the very intuition that is meant to direct you. Suppose you want to start a business doing something you love. You feel excited about it and begin to have some success and yet you hold a strong core belief that "you just can't trust people. Everyone is out to rip you off." What's your guess about what you'll end up creating? An employee who steals from you? A bookkeeper who embezzles your company's funds? Or perhaps a client who reneges on his agreement to pay for your product?

Intuition Exercise:
Belief Makeover Process

So how do you begin to turn around a negative core belief? First, it's necessary to become aware of this belief. It's not unconscious or invisible, as some people would have you think. Here are some questions to ask yourself:

Is there some situation that continually repeats in my life? For example:

A. Perhaps you're always finding yourself in a
   relationship with someone who cheats on you.
B. You continually have run-ins with authority figures.
C. You're always overlooked for a promotion at work.

Ask yourself, "What belief do I hold that might be causing this chronic situation?"

In the above examples a person who experiences A might hold the belief "You just can't trust men (or women)." The person who experiences B might hold a strong belief about their own lack of ability or education. Thus they need to "prove they are right" by experiencing conflict with authority figures. The person who experiences C might have the belief "I'll never get ahead. This is my lot in life."

Ask yourself, "Is this belief a fact or a perception?" Here's the tricky part: because you hold a strong belief about an issue, you are going to create it in your life. *Your belief will appear to be true.* The world around you will reinforce your belief. Part of the task in releasing a belief that no longer works for you is to begin to see it as a perception you have about your life. It's possible to change a perception. If you're willing to do this, you will create a profound change in your life.

Am I willing to change my belief? If so, what am I willing to change it to?

What outcome do you want to create? Changing a strong core belief isn't as easy as simply stating affirmations. Begin with small steps. Your task right now is to entertain the possibility that what you want to create is possible. Often when people try to do affirmations they take too big a leap. For example, if you're overwhelmed with credit card debt and you're trying to believe and affirm "I have an abundance of money," you probably won't succeed.

Be willing to say, "I believe it's possible to have . . ."

> . . . enough money.
> . . . a good relationship with my kids.
> . . . a healthy body.
> . . . a loving partner.
> . . . happy relationships with my peers.
> . . . work that I love.

What do *you* want? Ask your intuition for help. Imagine your intuition as your own personal cheerleading squad. Since you were born it has been with you, giving you encouraging messages like "You are worthy. Be willing to take a risk to do what you love. I am here for you. Here's an idea about how to proceed. Let me help you." It has communicated with you through images, dreams, words, ideas that pop into your head, physical sensations, and inner promptings. Can you grasp how hard it is for your intuition to help you when you're full of untruths such as "I'm not worthy; nothing good ever happens to me"? Be willing to change those thoughts and open up to the possibility that your life could be different, and I guarantee that your intuitive guidance system will respond with wild cheers and your life will begin to change for the better. When you shift your beliefs to allow for the possibility that you could have a life you love, you open up a channel of loving encouragement. Don't close it off. It's there to help you achieve success beyond your wildest dreams.

Your Intuition Journal

What beliefs do you hold that no longer work for you? Fill in the blanks below to get started. Don't *think* too much about the answers. Your first thought is probably the most accurate. You may find that you have positive beliefs in some areas and negative ones in another. Add some of your own.

> The world is . . .
> People are . . .
> My body is . . .
> Money is . . .
> Work is . . .
> I'll never . . .
> I'll always . . .
> Men are . . .
> Women are . . .
> The reason I can create a successful life is . . .
> I am willing to . . .
> The thing I'd most like to create in my life is . . .
> The five reasons I know I can do this are . . .
> What I've learned from this exercise is . . .

Was there anything you wrote that surprised you? We often make assumptions about the world that simply aren't true. After completing this exercise, look at the list to see if there are one or two beliefs you hold that no longer work for you. What belief would you like to hold instead?

LESSON 44

⸻ ◦◦◦ ⸻

Connecting with Spirit Every Day

*You are not a human being in search of
a spiritual experience. You are a spiritual
being immersed in a human experience.*

—Pierre Teilhard de Chardin

My client Mary Alice told me that she longed to be more spiritual. She wanted to feel God's presence in her life and to feel guided in all that she did throughout the day. "But," she sighed, "I go to church on holidays and say a quick prayer at night and that's about as close as I get to spiritual." I knew what she meant.

What does "being spiritual" mean to you? To many people it conjures up an image of a monk praying in a remote monastery. For others Mother Teresa may come to mind. If you tend toward New Age beliefs, you may ascribe the term *spiritual* to individuals who spend hours in silent meditation.

How do you connect with Spirit on a daily basis and still live in the real world of being a parent, going to work, and paying off the mortgage? Here are the words that come to mind when I think of someone who embodies spirituality.

Forgiving
Bighearted

Generous
Optimistic
Full of faith
Kind
Thoughtful
Patient
Loving
Slow to judge
Sees the best in people
Appreciative and grateful
Helpful to others
Takes time for prayer, silent communion, or meditation

Intuition Exercise:
Take Time for the Divine

Following are some suggestions for finding "Divine moments" to connect with the sacred in your daily life.

Morning blessings. Before you open your eyes in the morning, envision the day to come. Pray that you speak, think, and act with love and wisdom throughout the day.

Nature break. Take a few moments to step outside, rain or shine, and go for a short walk. You may see an unusual cloud formation, or a resilient weed pressing up through the pavement. You may feel inspired by the birds soaring in the sky, hear a child's laugh, or be especially appreciative of the clean air you breathe. Pay special attention to the natural beauty and abundance that God has created all around you.

Road peace. Most people don't behave in a raging and abusive manner when all is well in their lives. The Course in Miracles makes the statement "Today I will see all anger as a request for love." Imagine sending love to the harried driver who cut you off on your way to work. See him or her as needing your compassion rather than retaliation.

Gratitude pause. We spend much of our lives waiting, whether it's in line at the grocery store, in the elevator as we go to the office, or in the car in a traffic jam. Today when you find yourself with a few moments on your hands, think silent thoughts of gratitude for all that you have.

Angel blessings. You probably know someone at your office or in your neighborhood who is down on their luck. Perhaps they've been experiencing ill health, are caring for a sick family member, or have experienced a recent financial crisis. What could you provide that would be helpful to this person? Giving doesn't need to cost money. You could shovel a driveway, rake leaves, cook a meal, offer to baby-sit, drive them to a doctor's appointment, shop for their groceries, or simply provide a sympathetic ear.

Checkbook faith. Paying the bills each month creates anxiety for many people. Use it as an opportunity to build your faith by making a donation to someone less fortunate. Here's an affirmation to bring to mind as you write the check: "I freely give, knowing that as I do I am opening myself to God's rich abundance." There is a spiritual cycle of giving and receiving. As you freely give, you open yourself to receive.

Intuition interlude. The next time you find yourself fraught with anxiety, check in with your Divine guidance. Get in the habit of asking questions of your intuition and expecting a reply. "What could I do to feel calmer about the meeting this afternoon?" In response, you find an image coming to mind of a quiet lunch in the park by your office. One of the ways your intuition responds is through images. Your intuition is connected to a higher wisdom that always knows what you need. It will always lead you to peace, love, forgiveness, gratitude, and faith.

Your Intuition Journal

It's always helpful to define your goals. If you're seeking a deeper spiritual connection in your life, here are some questions to ask yourself.

What is your definition of *spiritual*?
Is there someone you know whom you consider spiritual?
What qualities do they embody that make them spiritual?
What are five things you could do to embrace Spirit in your own life?

When you bring the spiritual into your life, you begin to partner with a larger force. The Universe has your best interests at heart. It will forever encourage you toward success, prosperity, health, and love. Amazing things can and will unfold in your life when you partner with God.

LESSON 45

—◆—

Say "Yes" to What Enlivens You

*Put your self-care above anything else—saying no unless
it's an absolute yes, choosing to spend your time and
energy on things that bring you joy, and making decisions
based on what you want instead of what others want.
When you start practicing extreme self-care, a Divine
force rallies behind you to support your decisions.*

—Cheryl Richardson

My client Marsha dragged herself into my office last week and
began a litany of complaints. She told me about people who took
too much of her energy; her boss, who was extremely demanding;
and her endless volunteer activities that were no longer fun. I
have to confess that by the end of fifteen minutes I began to feel
exhausted myself. I stopped Marsha at that point. I spoke to her
about my belief that when you're consistently tired, drained,
bored, or anxious, these are clues from your intuition that something needs to be changed.

When a client has a consultation with me, I often view their
energy level. I sense through my inner guidance whether they are
in or out of the Divine flow of life force. When you do things that
give you energy—taking care of yourself, having fun, doing work
you love—the Divine current of life courses through you and

around you and you feel up and motivated. When you do things that drain you—experiencing constant feelings of worry, bitterness, anger, or resentment—you pinch yourself off from the flow. This results in low energy and exhaustion.

Marsha was so deeply entrenched in feelings of being overwhelmed and the perception that she was a victim of the situations she described that she couldn't easily identify what gave her energy. We decided to take her issues one at a time and come up with an action plan. Here is an example from Martha's session with me to assist you in coming up with your own plan.

Energy drain. I'm angry and upset at having to consistently work overtime at my job. My boss, Janet, seems to expect it because the department is understaffed.

What do you want? I need to know that there is a plan in place to hire more staff so I don't have to continue to work long hours. I want to be assured that I can have Wednesday evening off from work to attend the art class that I love.

Consult your inner guidance. Marsha decided the question she wanted to ask her intuition was, "What would make my work fun and enjoyable again?" She closed her eyes, took several deep breaths, and relaxed. Focusing inward, she allowed herself to feel open and receptive to any insights about her situation. I encouraged her to think about *receiving* an answer rather than actively *searching* for one. After five minutes she took another deep breath, exhaled, and opened her eyes. She looked relieved and had a smile on her face.

Results. During the brief meditation, Marsha came to understand that Janet was just as overwhelmed as she was and was not someone who readily offered acknowledgment. This gave her the slight shift in perception she needed to not feel like a victim in her work situation. Marsha wanted to stay at this company but decided she needed more information from her boss about the plans to hire more staff.

Action steps. Based on the above information, Marsha set up a meeting to speak to Janet the next day. Much to Marsha's surprise, Janet was pleased that she had taken the initiative to arrange the time to talk. Her boss assured her that there was a plan in place to reduce her workload and readily agreed to make sure Marsha would not have to work late on Wednesdays.

The above is a good model to use when you're feeling stuck in a rut or simply finding yourself more tired than usual. Get in the habit of asking yourself intuition questions such as "What do I want?" "What's the best possible outcome?" "What would make me feel better right now?" and "What steps could I take to bring about the situation I want?" The best plan is one that you have some control over. Steer clear of answers that involve forcing someone else to do it your way. Divine Intuition always presents options that are win-win solutions for all involved.

Make a conscientious effort to:
Say "yes" to thoughts of gratitude.
Say "yes" to taking care of yourself.
Say "yes" to people or situations that enliven you.
Say "yes" to anonymous, random acts of kindness.
Say "yes" to activities you most enjoy.
Say "yes" to doing something just outside of your normal comfort zone.
Say "yes" to doing things that increase your self-esteem.
Say "yes" to taking small steps toward a goal.
Say "yes" to taking a risk.
Say "yes" to speaking your truth to someone.
Say "yes" to thoughts of forgiveness.
Say "yes" to fun.
Say "yes" to trusting your still, small inner voice.
Say "yes" to spending time in nature.

Say "yes" to telling someone you love them.

Say "yes" to opening up communication with someone who hurt you.

Say "yes" to doing something nice for yourself every day.

Intuition Exercise: Reenergize!

Energy drain. Write several paragraphs in your journal describing what you're upset about. Who or what is taking your energy?

What do you want? Think about what would feel great in this situation. What provides you with a sense of relief when you think about it? That's a clue from your intuition about the outcome you need to move toward. Describe it.

Consult your inner guidance. Close your eyes and take a deep breath. Imagine being filled and surrounded by a feeling of love. Ask for Divine guidance to assist you. (Pause.) Ask the question, "What can I do to change this situation to a more positive one?" (Or substitute your own question.) Continue to remain open and expansive. Allow the information to come to you. A thought may pop into your mind. You might have a sudden shift in perception, or you might see the problem from another perspective. (Pause.) Stay in this altered consciousness until you feel ready to end. (Pause.) Open your eyes and write down your answers.

Results. You may not receive the information immediately. Be willing to sit with the question for the rest of the day. The answer from your intuition may come to you when you least expect it. If you did receive an answer, write it down.

Action steps. What steps are indicated? Do you need to clarify something with someone? Speak your truth? Let go of something or someone? See a situation from a different perspective or simply be willing to wait something out? You may also receive an answer that indicates that you need to do more things that are fun and enjoyable. What steps are you willing to take?

Your Intuition Journal

Are you feeling overwhelmed? If so, the thought of taking time to figure out how to reduce your stress may at first seem to add to the pressure. However, it's a vital step. Take five minutes and write down a strategy for relief by answering the following questions.

What are the top four priorities in your life at this time?
Is there any area that is consistently out of balance?
What steps could you take to remedy this?

Write down at least one thing that you could do today or this week to give yourself a reprieve from the stress. If you sigh with relief when you think about having completed this task, that's your intuition saying, "Yes!" Now go do it!

LESSON 46

Learning to Trust the Process

*Sometimes it is like a tiny voice in the wilderness;
at other times it is loud, clear, and direct. When
we learn to stop, listen, and follow the guidance
that it provides, we experience bliss, or at the
very least, a deep sense of personal fulfillment.*

—Hal Zina Bennett

I've known my client Pam for about eight years, and throughout that time she's been through incredible highs and absolute lows in her life. She's survived a life-threatening illness, the loss of a business, and years of legal disputes, and yet she remains amazingly resilient. What's her secret? She knows that when one of her dreams dies, she'll create a new and better one to take its place.

Our culture thrives on instant gratification. Have you ever had a new idea or a new goal and wanted to have it manifested yesterday?! Many people are like that. Through Pam and others, I've had the opportunity to learn to begin to appreciate and trust the process by which our dreams become reality.

Your hopes and dreams are one of the ways your intuition communicates with you. When you try something and it doesn't work, too often you may quit. You decide that your dream wasn't really in the stars, you had bad karma, or it was just one of the proverbial "learning experiences" you keep hearing about. What happens is that you become impatient and you give up.

Has this happened to you? You had a goal, you tried to make it happen, it didn't work out the way you imagined it would, and so you stopped trying. And worst of all, in your disappointment, you stopped dreaming.

It's often difficult for me to work with someone who no longer has any hopes and dreams. They literally feel "hopeless." They begin to settle for what they think they can achieve rather than what they want to achieve. They begin to keep their dreams realistic, practical, and uninspiring. They begin to settle for less and less, and they finally stop dreaming. Why bother?

One of the world's greatest inventors, Thomas Edison, said, "I am not discouraged, because every wrong attempt discarded is another step forward." He knew what it was like to try and fail over and over again. Yet because he persisted in his dream, he changed the way we live with a thousand patented inventions, including the phonograph and the light bulb.

Never, ever stop dreaming! Your dreams are a primary way you receive guidance from your Spirit. Pay attention to what makes you soar. Some dreams will prove disappointing, and you may reach a few dead ends, but don't give up. Keep dreaming and finding new ways to rekindle your energy and enthusiasm.

Your dreams and visions are your connection with your life mission, or what you are here to accomplish. It's important to understand that part of the assignment you came here to take on is not simply the achievement of your goals. It's to walk the path to your dreams with love, patience, kindness, forgiveness, and respect for yourself and others. Your dreams empower you. Make sure you dream big dreams!

Intuition Exercise:
Be Receptive to Your Dreams

Sit quietly and close your eyes. Allow your mind to drift back to a time in your past when you had a burning desire or dream you wanted to fulfill. Perhaps it was to have a family, to own your own home, to have a certain type of career, or to obtain a college degree.

Spend a few minutes communing with this younger you. What were your hopes, dreams, and ambitions five, ten, fifteen, twenty years ago? How did you know what you wanted to achieve? How did it feel? What did it look like? How did you experience it in your body? These are all ways your intuition communicates your true passions and purpose.

Allow your thoughts to move forward in time. What became of those hopes and dreams? Did you allow some of them to fall away through discouragement? Did a few of them come true? Perhaps some of your dreams changed along the way as you grew and matured.

Most of our goals do not materialize overnight. They take months, years, and sometimes decades to mature and manifest. Look at one of the dreams that you have achieved and look at the process you've gone through to succeed. What have you learned? What are you proud of? What do you wish you had done differently?

Take a slow, deep breath and exhale. Ask your Higher Power, "What new dreams should I pursue?" Wait, listen, and reflect on the answer you receive. (Pause.)

Then ask, "I want to allow this dream to unfold with joy, ease, and peace—how may I begin?"

Your Intuition Journal

Achieving a long-held dream is exhilarating. It increases your self-esteem and heightens your sense of purpose. It also gives you the self-confidence to move ahead to even bigger achievements.

List five things you're proud of achieving.

What did you learn about yourself through their accomplishment?

What was the most difficult thing you experienced while fulfilling these dreams?

Have you ever felt that you stopped just short of achieving a goal?

If so, what do you wish you had done differently?

What promise will you make to yourself as you seek to follow your new dreams?

If you have difficulty feeling motivated about the topic of pursuing your dreams, it's okay to think small. Your intuition leads you on the path to happiness step by step. The answers may not present themselves through a strong passion, but they may lie in an aptitude, interest, or simple knowing.

LESSON 47

Affirmations That Work

*Within you right now is the power to do things you
never dreamed possible. This power becomes available
to you just as soon as you can change your beliefs.*

—Maxwell Maltz

I received a letter last week written in a very formal tone with spidery, cramped handwriting. It began, "Dear Mrs. Robinson, I wish to inform you that affirmations do not work. I have made it my duty to notify anyone suggesting otherwise that they are wrong." I wasn't quite sure how to respond at the time, and even if I could, I realized, the letter writer had not given me a return address. This chapter is directed to Anna, wherever she is.

Dear Anna: Affirmations are clear, positive statements about what you would like to create in your life. Most of us would like to have health, wealth, love, joy, good relations with our fellow human beings, work that we enjoy, a belief system or philosophy of life that gives our lives hope and meaning, as well as a close-knit group of friends and family. We wish this for ourselves and hopefully we wish it for others. Affirmations are an attempt to enlist the power of words, beliefs, hopes, and an inexplicable something larger than ourselves to come to our aid and help us create new outcomes in our lives. Here are some guidelines:

What do you want? You may want to take your journal and brainstorm for a few pages, writing about your ideal life circumstances. Many people continue to focus on what they *don't* want. "I don't want to be poor" or "I don't want a boyfriend who cheats on me." Begin simply by maintaining the focus on what you want to create.

Affirmations are written in the present tense. If your intention is to create a new job and increase your income, you might affirm, "My work is fun and creative and I am paid well for it." Some people choose affirmations that are all-encompassing, such as, "I feel balanced, joy-filled, healthy, and happy."

Don't try to figure out how you'll reach your goal. When you maintain your focus on what you want, your intuition will immediately begin to give you clues about how to reach your goals. Your task is to awake each day determined to follow what you feel excited and enthusiastic about. Tough job description! Your Higher Power will begin to orchestrate all that is necessary to bring about your goal. Stay alert for synchronicities and coincidences. They indicate that you're on the right track and that your goal is within reach. Make your affirmation and let the Universe take care of the details.

Affirmations are about you, not someone else. I once had a client who was involved with a man who was nervous about making a commitment. He would frequently break up with her and then want to get back together again. She told me her affirmation was "George will marry me." I explained that true affirmations are not about getting someone else to change. After some discussion we agreed that what she wanted was to affirm, "I am in a loving, happy, and committed relationship." I heard from her a year later. She had finally ended the relationship with George and was happily engaged to someone else.

Your affirmation should make you feel at peace. Affirmations shouldn't be hard work; nor should they make you feel anxious. If you experience a contradiction every time you say your affirmation, then you need to change it to something that doesn't produce that reaction. For example, if you want to create more wealth and prosperity in your life at a time when you feel quite poor, it will not help to constantly be affirming, "I am rich!" Instead choose words that are soothing, such as, "I am open and receptive to new avenues of income." Doesn't that feel better?

Intuition Exercise:
Treasure Your Life

Some people have a difficult time figuring out what they want. If you're one of those people, this is a great exercise for you. It's called a "treasure map." It's a visual representation of what you want to create in your life.

To begin, gather a dozen or so old magazines and lay them out in front of you. Travel, home design, and gardening magazines are my favorites.

Look through each issue, selecting and cutting out images that inspire you. They might be pictures of places you want to travel to or a room that is evocative of a style you'd like to create. Perhaps it's a representation of two people in love.

Look for words that make you feel good, and cut those out as well. I also like to include something that represents the spiritual in my treasure map. This might be a picture of an angel or the sun streaming through trees.

When you're finished, paste the images and words on a poster or pin them to a corkboard. Put your creation in a place where you'll see it frequently. I have my current map positioned over my desk. I love to look at it every day because it makes me feel happy. I have a small banner over the whole thing that says, "My intuition guides me. I live my life in love, ease, and harmony. My future is glorious." May it be so for you, too.

Your Intuition Journal

Many people waste far too much energy endlessly analyzing a past failure. They ask, "What went wrong?" or "What should I have done differently?" It's much more productive to put your focus on what went well and what contributed to your success. Following are some questions for your journal.

Think of a time in your life when you achieved a goal easily and effortlessly.

> What contributed to your success? Was there a state of mind you achieved? A positive expectation? A willingness to take a risk?

> Write about something you would like to create in your life right now.

> Write an affirmation that will assist you in achieving this goal.

Do you feel good when you say your affirmation to yourself? Does it give you a boost of confidence? If you find your thoughts beginning to drift back to old failures, consciously shift your attention to the successes you've written about in this journal exercise and focus on the positive feeling you receive when you say your affirmation.

LESSON 48

———◉———

Replenish Your Spirit

For fast-acting relief, try slowing down.

—Lily Tomlin

I belong to something called a Master Mind Group. It is essentially a group of professionals who meet monthly to support one another's personal and professional growth. The structure is fairly consistent and is divided into three parts. First, we each take time to talk about our successes in the past month. Then we ask for ideas and suggestions as we discuss any challenges we may be experiencing. Finally, each of us makes a commitment to a personal or professional goal that we will achieve by the next session. A wonderful woman named Jane hosts my group.

The goal part comes very easily to me. By the end of each session I've usually scribbled a page of notes about various things I want to accomplish and complete. At the appointed time in our last meeting I told the group what my main goal was for the next month. I was met with silence. . . . Then Jane said, "Lynn, I think you need to go on a retreat." I looked around at the other members, who were all nodding in silent agreement. "Oh no," I thought, "I've become one of those women who never takes time for herself." It got me to take a serious look at my beliefs about how to create a life I love and the value in slowing down.

I decided to go on a one-day prayer retreat at a local seminary. While I was there I came to understand (again) that I didn't have to become a "human doing." I could slow down, have fun as a human *being*, and use my mind and my imagination to create my goals and desires.

Intuition Exercise:
Mini-Retreat Secrets

Here are some of the ideas that came to me on my retreat:

Each day take a conscious mini-spiritual retreat. This doesn't have to involve large amounts of time. It can simply be sitting outside and listening to the birds sing or closing your eyes for a few minutes to focus on your breath as you slowly inhale and exhale. I also find that listening to inspirational music can be very calming.

Make daily exercise a must. You don't need a membership at the local gym to commit to this. What kind of activity did you like to do when you were a kid? I love to dance. It makes my heart soar. I also love to go for long walks in the woods. These feel like Spirit-filled times to me. What's fun for you?

Pay attention to your energy. When my last book came out, I found I was consistently doing things that I thought I *should* do in order to promote it. I felt constantly overwhelmed and hassled. When I began to simply focus on the things that were fun about promoting my book, everything began to fall into place and the book sales took off.

Keep a long-term perspective. Patience was not something I was born with. I've had to work at it. One of the things I learned on my retreat was that I unreasonably expected all my goals to happen quickly. When they didn't I began to doubt myself, and question whether I could achieve the success I desired. I had to train myself to take a long-term perspective.

Cultivate a sense of humor. During my retreat I realized I had been taking many things in my life far too seriously. It was time to lighten up! When I returned I began to rent comedy videos and read humorous books. It was amazing what a difference a simple change in perspective made.

Your Intuition Journal

Going to a spa or traveling to a retreat can be expensive. If your lifestyle allows it, definitely make space for these activities. However, with a little creativity you can inexpensively re-create some of these experiences in your life. Think of taking this time as a daily commitment to nurturing your soul, your body, and your mind.

If going to the gym is not your idea of a good time, what kind of exercise is fun for you to do? For example: dancing, swimming, walking the dog, canoeing, cross-country skiing.

How could you incorporate more of these activities into your everyday life? For example: could you start a neighborhood walking group, or hire yourself out as a dog walker?

What are three things you could implement that would allow you to feel pampered? For example: designate one evening of the week as "take-out food night," exchange manicures with a girlfriend, or create a meditation group.

What does your spirit long for? What's the first thought that comes to mind? Write that down!

While pampering yourself may strike many as a bit frivolous, it's important to honor your body as the temple of your spirit. When you slow down and cherish life, your soul appreciates it, and so will you.

───※◎※───

Moving Through Life Transitions

> *Between letting go (of the old) and successfully*
> *launching the new there is a time of confusion and*
> *emptiness. People often feel lost during this time, and*
> *too often they interpret that lostness as yet another sign*
> *that something is wrong. It is simply a sign that they*
> *have entered the fertile chaos of the neutral zone.*
>
> —William Bridges

I don't know many people who love going through life transitions. About 90 percent of the calls I receive for intuitive consultations are from people who are contemplating a career change, beginning or ending a relationship, or coping with a tangible or intangible loss of some kind in their life. I frequently hear people telling me that they're "stuck" or "in a rut," and yet most are in that limbo state called transition.

Transition often feels like being lost in the woods. There seem to be no obvious markers that say, "This way to safety." If you look up the word *transition* in the dictionary, you'll see definitions like "passing from one state to another" and references to "transformation," "passage," "major change," "shift," or "development." Even though you may feel stuck, these words indicate movement and change. Sometimes it seems there is no apparent progress toward your hopes and dreams. You feel scared that you're falling apart and might be in this "no place" forever. You feel stalled, and yet often it's that uncomfortable shift from one place in your life to the next where the most growth occurs.

When I'm in this transition zone and fear that nothing is happening, I find comfort in the example of tulips. You plant them in the fall and they come up in the spring. In the intervening months, there appears to be nothing going on. You wouldn't think of digging them up in the middle of winter and yelling at them that they're "stuck" and admonishing them to "grow faster!" They are doing exactly what they need to do. And when all the circumstances needed for their flowering occur, they appear and bloom. The same is true for your transitions. The wisdom that guides the flowers guides your life as well.

Everyone experiences transitions many times during the course of a lifetime. It feels unpleasant because it requires that you let go of the known, the familiar, what you've come to think of as safe. You know where you've been, but you don't know where you're headed. Many people deal with this discomfort by trying to go back to the old. It's like trying to stuff the toothpaste back in the tube. You want the old job back or you attempt to reestablish a relationship that is no longer viable. When you feel bored, restless, or out of sorts, it's a call from your intuition that it's time for a change. You call on your Higher Power to help you, and it responds with encouragement to release the old to make room for the new.

We hear of people trying to "cope" with change. That word implies struggle. If at all possible, try to embrace change. The author Margaret Drabble wrote, "When nothing is sure, everything is possible." The fact that you're uncomfortable doesn't mean you're doing something wrong. It just means that change is happening and you—like most people—feel anxious when it occurs. This transition zone can be a very creative time. Your life is up in the air, but anything and everything is possible.

The Universe is helping you move the old, resistant places in yourself to allow something new, fresh, and invigorating to take its place. I've found that as difficult as it is, the most helpful attitude is to embrace the transition. The one true thing about transitions is that they have an end. You will land on solid ground once more. It will just be in a different place than you've ever been before. There's an old saying: "When everything is breaking up, something new is breaking through."

Times of transition are a study in contradictions. At the point you want to rail at the Universe for causing this change in your life, you also need to trust the wisdom of this same force to bring about the transformation you need. Intuition is extremely helpful in transition, as it will point the way to the path that will take you to your new life. However, it's also challenging to attempt to find a balance between taking time to listen to your intuition and taking action to put your inner guidance into motion. Victor Hugo said this well: "Have courage for the great sorrows of life, and patience for the small ones; and when you have laboriously accomplished your daily task, go to sleep in peace. God is awake."

Intuition Exercise:
Directions for Crossing the Bridges of Life

Be patient. Transitions usually have a rhythm and a timing all their own. It's very tempting to "do something—anything." That course of action usually gets you into a deeper crisis. Trust that there is deep change happening within your psyche that is providing the information and impetus to propel you to the next stage in your life. It can't—and shouldn't—be rushed by a hasty decision.

Allow downtime. What brings you comfort? Is it a quiet walk, doing needlepoint, cooking a favorite meal, listening to music, petting your dog, sitting quietly in your backyard? Intuitive guidance flourishes during those quiet times when your mind is not actively engaged in planning and worry.

Find support. Do you know a good listener you can talk with? You don't necessarily need advice. You want someone who can ask open-ended questions, listen to your answers without judgment, and allow you to find your own way. Is there a good friend, relative, therapist, neighbor, minister, or rabbi who might be able to help?

Remember. You've gone through transitions before and made it to the other side. The present you're so comfortable with now may once have been a terrifying journey into the unknown. What did you do that helped you get through it? A sense of loss and grief, feelings of confusion and anxiety, and tears are all normal parts of the process. Just know that you can do it again.

Pray and ask for guidance. You may be tempted to petition God for the life you had before: "Please, God, give me back my old job." It might be helpful to try a new kind of prayer—asking for strength, courage, patience, clarity, wisdom, peace of mind, and faith. These are the qualities that will get you through any of life's difficulties. Ask to be shown the path to your highest good, or a vision of the new life you're moving toward.

Focus on the positive. What are the benefits of this change that's taken place in your life? Perhaps you have time for a new hobby, lunch with friends, the freedom to be with your kids or your spouse, the ability to take a course you've always been interested in. Is there something you've wanted to try but haven't had the time to pursue? Those sparks of interest are clues from your intuition about the direction to take. Indulge yourself.

Go on a retreat. The simpler, the better. Perhaps you have a friend who has a vacation home that you could use in the off-season. Maybe you could rent a cottage for a few days that's a short distance from your home. The idea is to get away from the influence of your normal surroundings. Take a journal with you and begin to write about your recent past and your dreams for the future. Don't feel that you need to write the great American novel. You're simply there to cultivate a sense of openness, curiosity, and wonder. Allow yourself to be an open vessel into which the Universe can pour its wisdom.

Use your imagination. It might be helpful to close your eyes and imagine yourself at some future date looking back on this time in your life. Ask that future self how it can help you through this particular life transition. Is there anything that the future self wishes the younger self had known or done differently? You may feel that you're making this up, but if the information is useful and helps you experience a greater sense of peace, use it to your advantage!

Your Intuition Journal

Try a free-writing style in answering these two journal questions. Don't *think* about them too much. Just answer from your heart.

> What do you need to let go of?
> What's next in your life?

Times of change don't have to be difficult and painful. Use this period of time when you feel like you're "between things" to have fun, to be creative and even a wee bit impulsive!

LESSON 50

Be Willing to Take Risks

Every morning, when we wake up, we have twenty-four brand-new hours to live. What a precious gift! We have the capacity to live in a way that these twenty-four hours will bring peace, joy, and happiness to ourselves and others.

—Thich Nhat Hanh

I remember the exact moment I thought about risk taking for the first time in my life. I was ten years old, playing in my backyard by myself, when I received what I can only describe as a bolt of Divine guidance. It came out of the blue. It was a thought that stopped me in my tracks. One minute I was playing and the next moment I just knew that my life had been transformed. An inner voice said, "You have a choice about whether you play it safe in your life. If you choose to take risks, to confront and walk through your fears, you will be able to achieve all that you dream."

Pretty heavy stuff for a ten-year-old! But I knew exactly what the voice meant. I knew that I had an option to live life small and safe, but I also knew that if I chose the path of living life large I would have all the help, guidance, and direction I needed to succeed. You can make the same decision. You have a unique purpose you have come here to accomplish. You don't have to take huge risks. You don't have to find the cure for AIDS or found a new religion. But to live a fuller, more passionate life, you must learn to trust your intuition to be your friend and guide.

If I had waited until I was totally confident before I left my job to begin an intuitive-consulting business, it wouldn't have happened. If I had waited until I was 100 percent sure I could write a book before I signed the contract, I wouldn't have done it. Taking a risk is about knowing you have to move out of your comfort zone and become a bigger person. President Teddy Roosevelt said, "Do what you can, with what you have, where you are."

I grew up during the 1960s. There was a huge revolution to bring about peace on earth. We may still need a revolution, but not necessarily the outer kind. It's the inner kind. You are here to create peace within yourself and allow those waves of calmness, love, forgiveness, and kindness to flow out into the world. The Universe may be a huge place, but there are no small actions and no small thoughts. Everything is interconnected; everything matters. *You* can be the change you want to see in the world.

The Universe gives you those dreams in order for you to become the best person you can be. You deserve to take that risk. Is it scary? *Yes!* The first three months after I started my business I would sit in my office and cry before my clients came in. I was sure that someone would discover I was a total fake! When I was asked to give my first speech, I had a muscle spasm in my back for two solid weeks before the event.

Do I still feel scared? Yes. The only difference now is that I *know* absolutely that the Universe is there to guide me. It doesn't put anything in my path that I can't handle. I make a conscious choice to feel calm. I simply affirm, "I can do this. I am supported. I'll know what I need to do when I need to do it." Knowing that allows me to accept change with more grace and without the extremes of anxiety that I once experienced. I know that events may not unfold exactly as I want. But whatever happens, I'll be fine.

Don't fall into the trap of imagining that everything has to be perfect. It never will be. Your task is to figure out what you want. After that, allow the Universe to begin bringing together the resources necessary for you to have your dream. Then it's time for you to take a leap of faith and go for your dream. Don't imagine that any of the heroes or heroines you look up to hasn't gone through this same process. They have! They've all been scared as they looked out over the chasm they needed to leap across.

Marianne Williamson put this so succinctly when she said, "Our deepest fear is not that we are inadequate. Our deepest fear is that we are powerful beyond measure. It is our light, not our darkness that most frightens us. Who are we *not* to be brilliant, gorgeous, talented and fabulous? You are a child of God. Your playing small doesn't serve the world. We were born to make manifest the glory of God that is within us. It's not just in some of us; it's in us all."

In order to create a life you love, you need to take risks. I'm not talking about the leaping-off-a-cliff-with-a-bungee-cord-attached type of risk, or marching into your boss's office and saying, "I quit." (Unless you feel strongly guided to do so!) I'm speaking about the small risks that will move you out of your comfort zone. It might be calling someone you feel intimidated by, increasing the fees for a service you provide, or agreeing to chair a project for your kid's school.

Everyone has a different set of circumstances that make up their comfort zone. When you choose to move out of the perceived safety of the known and into the unknown, miracles will begin to occur. With each risk you take, you'll start to feel more and more comfortable. You'll find that the Universe will start to deliver your dreams to you more quickly. Your self-confidence and self-esteem will improve and you'll begin to feel powerful. Your vision of yourself and what you can achieve in the world will begin to expand. As you become bigger, you'll find that you can hold a vision of what you want to achieve, and before you know it, success will be yours. You already have more power than you can imagine! Begin to own it. It will provide you with enormous energy to create your dreams.

Intuition Exercise:
Take a Risk a Day

Your intuition will constantly place new ideas in front of you in order to assist you in reaching your goals. Of course, you always have a choice to act on these ideas or not. Take a risk a day in order to expand your comfort zone. Think about the goals you have in various areas of your life and think of a risk you could take in any of the following areas that are important to you:

Friends: for example, I'm going to call Ron and ask if he'd like to have coffee with me.

Family: for example, I'm going to tell my brother that I love and forgive him.

Health: for example, I'm going to make an appointment with the doctor to discuss the symptoms I'm concerned about.

Professional: for example, I'm going to set up a meeting with my boss to discuss my ideas about the department.

Personal: for example, I'm calling Sandy to ask if she'll be my walking partner so that I'll commit to a daily walk.

Spiritual: for example, I'm going to sign up for the prayer retreat at my church.

Write about your choices and feel free to add categories not listed above.

Write down seven risks in your journal. Before you go to sleep each night, think about the risk you'll be taking tomorrow. Visualize it clearly and rehearse it in your mind. See a successful outcome. Ask God for whatever help you need. "Dear God: Please fill me with courage tomorrow as I ask my boss for a raise. Help me to be articulate and strong. Remind me how powerful and deserving I am. Amen."

Your Intuition Journal

We all have a "risk-taking style." The spectrum of styles can vary from someone who is totally risk averse to a person who seems to thrive on danger. Eleanor Roosevelt suggested that you should "do one thing every day that scares you." The journal questions listed here are to help you evaluate whether or not your style works for you.

What risks have you taken in the past?
Have your risks resulted in a better situation?
If yes, describe.
If no, describe what you feel you could have done differently.
What could you do in order to feel secure enough to take risks again?
Describe two bigger risks you'd like to take later this year.

If thinking about risk has you running for cover, you might consider the words of Olympic gold medalist Brian Goodell, who said, "We all experience doubts and fears as we approach new challenges. The fear diminishes with the confidence that comes from experience and faith. Sometimes you just have to go for it and see what happens. Jumping into the battle does not guarantee victory, but being afraid to try guarantees defeat."

LESSON 51

⊸◉⊸

Qualities of Your Spirit

*Within every soul there is a rose. The God-like qualities
planted in us at birth grow amid the thorns of our faults.
Many of us look at ourselves and see only the thorns, the
effects. We despair, thinking that nothing good can possibly
come from us. We neglect to water the good within us,
and eventually it dies. We never realize our potential.*

—author unknown

Whom do you most admire? When I think about the answer to
that question a whole host of people pop into my mind. I admire
my friend Cheryl for her courage, Laura for her integrity, Mimi for
her creative ideas, John for his sensitivity, Gail for her generosity,
Gary for his warmth and enthusiasm, and Michael for his humor.
Your Spirit led you to connect with the people on *your* list to help
you learn from their qualities. These may be people you know in
real life or simply admire from afar. But what you appreciate and
respect in others are often qualities you identify with and wish to
emulate.

In all this talk about designing the life we want we often focus
on the tangible: What *kind* of job? What *brand* of car? How *much*
money? And we forget about the qualities we want to develop:
honesty, patience, virtue, kindness, and compassion, which will

aid us in achieving our life goals. We speak of accomplishing our life desires and we hope that once we get them we will be perfect, set, and satisfied forever. But our Higher Self has other plans. The Universe uses our desires to help us develop the soul qualities we are here on earth to learn.

I believe that one of my biggest lessons is learning patience. For example, writing and publishing a book has been an amazing instruction process in being patient. I wait for the words to come, for the chapter to be completed, to find an agent, to find a publisher, to have the editor edit my words, to have the book be printed, for reviewers to write about what I've written, and finally I wait for the readers who want to buy and read my book. From start to finish, a book project can take years. What I understand through my intuition is that my task is to learn to enjoy each step, to relish the stages of the process, rather than simply achieving the goal.

I'm also aware that my difficulty with patience has had an interesting flip side—an advantage, if you will. It's made me more of a risk taker. I've often joked that I've gotten where I am because I leap before I look! It's also helped me trust my intuition. "Why wait around?" I ask myself. "If it feels right, I do it!" And usually things work out for the best.

Many of the qualities you're reading this book to work on have an advantage for you as well. I have a friend who will confess that she is often intolerant and judgmental. She recognizes this and is vigilant about trying to develop her compassion. However, the thing that I love most about her is her honesty. I know that she'll tell me the truth when no one else will. She's forthright and direct and doesn't equivocate about the facts. I find her refreshing to be around. (Although not when I'm feeling thin-skinned!)

What about you? When you think about the difficulties you've experienced in your life, do you see the thread of a persistent lesson you may be here to learn? Can you also see how that challenge has made you stronger, or possibly aided you in developing a positive, more spiritual attribute, such as compassion or kindness? In his book *We Are God*, author Deena Naidu writes, "Let Compassion be your right arm, Tolerance be your left, Service be your right leg and Goodwill be the left. Let Love be your upper torso and Truth be your lower. Let Kindness be your right foot and Courage be your left. With all these as part of your makeup, how can you ever be less than Divine?"

We are all here to learn. This schoolroom called earth is a wonderful and miraculous place. It continues to offer us opportunities to open our hearts, to love others as well as ourselves, and to connect with Spirit to find our way home.

Intuition Exercise:
Who Would You Like to Be?

Following is a list of some common qualities.

1. Circle the qualities that you already have.
2. Put a checkmark next to the qualities you would like to develop.

Ambition	Appreciation of nature	Appreciation of others
Artistry	Charity	Compassion
Competence	Courage	Creativity
Curiosity	Dependability	Determination
Devotion to career	Devotion to environment	Devotion to family
Diligence	Discretion	Empathy
Enthusiasm	Experience	Expressiveness
Flexibility	Foresight	Friendliness
Generosity	Gentleness	Handiness

Healing	Humility	Humor
Imagination	Insightfulness	Integrity
Intelligence	Intuition	Kindness
Leadership	Loyalty	Negotiation
Organization	Patience	Perseverance
Physical fitness	Precision	Resourcefulness
Sensitivity	Softness	Spirituality
Strength	Stylishness	Talent
Thoughtfulness	Warmth	Whimsicality

3. What areas of your life are easy because of the qualities you circled?

4. What areas of your life are difficult because of the qualities you checked?

5. Think of a difficult time in your life. Briefly describe it in your journal.

6. What quality do you think your Divine Intuition may have been trying to help you learn through your experience during this difficult time?

7. As you experiment with qualities you'd like to develop, try the "as if" technique. Act as if you already have it! When you can do that on a regular basis, you'll discover you're halfway there!

Your Intuition Journal

You may seem to have been born with some qualities because they come easily to you. Others you have to work at developing.

Was there anything that surprised you in the qualities you either circled or checked above?

What qualities would you most like to develop?

What could you do that would enable you to do this?

Is there someone who has an abundance of a particular quality that you'd like to develop? Consider having a conversation with them. Encourage them to talk about their philosophy of life. You might find that their way of thinking and feeling rubs off on you!

The Best Is Yet to Come

We come equipped with everything we need to experience a powerful life full of joy, incredible passion, and profound peace. The difficult part is giving ourselves the permission to live it.

—Deborah Rosado Shaw

Part of living a passionate life is to get in the habit of dreaming big. What happens when your dream finally arrives? You're offered the job you always wanted. The book contract gets signed. You have an opportunity to speak on national television about your product or service. You've met the man (or woman) of your dreams. The last of your kids leaves home for college and your life is finally yours. Wow! You've finally made it! This is bliss, right? But why does it feel so scary?

When success finally arrives at our doorstep, very few of us feel ready for it. Why? There's an odd process that takes place as we begin to achieve success and expand our life plans. We have to grow bigger inside. Our self-confidence and self-respect have to develop and match the life vision we dreamed about. Life is a process. It's not just about achieving goals. A loving Spirit who wants us to grow in faith, love, and courage constantly pushes us just beyond our comfort zone. We have to grow into our new dreams.

It's normal to feel scared and uncertain. When my first book, *The Complete Idiot's Guide to Being Psychic*, came out I did all the things I've written about in this book. I wanted the book to be success-ful, so I prayed, visualized, affirmed, listened to my intuition, took small steps and big actions. One day I received a call from what I thought was a local television affiliate. They wanted to tape a brief interview with me. "Great!" I thought. "My goals are being achieved!" That thought was immediately followed by abject fear. I cried. I felt paralyzed by concern over what to wear. I felt too fat. What if I flubbed an answer or, worse yet, blanked out and noth-ing would come out of my mouth? On the one hand, I knew I had to go to the interview; on the other hand, I wished that it were anyone other than me being interviewed.

I prepared by having my friends conduct practice interviews. During the fake interviews I would dissolve into tears at odd mo-ments. Finally, the day of the actual interview arrived. Wearing a new outfit and still feeling less than confident, I arrived at my office, where the camera crew was setting up. I then learned that the station wasn't a Boston affiliate; my interview was being taped for an international news audience! I wanted to die. My inner voice was practically chanting in my ear, "Fake it until you make it!" It was the only thing I could think to do. "How would a con-fident person act right now?" I asked myself. I straightened my shoulders, held my head high, and sailed through the interview like a pro. It wasn't until I got home that I began crying again. This time they were tears of relief.

I'm telling you this anecdote because I know you will experience your own variation of this story as you begin to follow your dreams. Everyone who has achieved a dream has had to walk an uncom-fortable bridge in order to get from the "safe" side to the riches waiting for them on the opposite side. There is good news, how-ever: it gets better and easier each time. Now when I'm asked for an interview, I feel calm, cool, and collected. I actually *look forward* to the event. It doesn't feel scary or intimidating anymore. I like being on stage! The confidence, self-respect, and self-esteem that have come to me as the result of walking through the fire of doubt and fear have freed me to create a life I love. I can dream bigger dreams and know that, with time, I'll achieve them.

You have a choice about the kind of life you want to create. Will there be setbacks, fear, and confusion on your path? Absolutely. However, when most of your hours and days are characterized by joy, love, hope, courage, and passion, you'll know you're on the right track. This poem by Robert Frost seems like a great place to end . . . and begin:

> I shall be telling this with a sigh
> Somewhere ages and ages hence:
> Two roads diverged in a wood, and I—
> I took the one less traveled by,
> And that has made all the difference.

When you find that path, keep walking and don't look back, because the best is yet to come.

Intuition Exercise:
The Life You Were Meant to Live

Close your eyes and imagine sitting in a beautiful garden filled with golden light. (Pause.) All around you are the teachers, guides, and angels who assist you on your path. You are at your graduation ceremony. (Pause.) Feel their love, which fills and surrounds you. (Pause.) Everyone is pleased at your progress. (Pause.) A beautiful, rich red carpet has been laid out in front of you. At the end of this carpet are some steps, and at the top of the steps stands your inner guide. Your guide is holding a golden necklace with a beautiful radiant star. As you walk up the steps to stand before your guide, the necklace is placed over your head and the star pendant falls gracefully over your heart. (Pause.) You are told that the star is the key to help you unlock all of your potential. Whenever you need wise counsel, you only have to think of this necklace and know that the answers will come. You are not alone.

See yourself moving to any of the other guides and angels who have a message for you at this time. Stand before them and ask for their wise guidance. Imagine feeling their love for you fill your entire being with a surge of energy. (Pause.) Know that even if you can't hear the answers, your soul is receiving the response it needs. (Pause.) You feel filled with gratitude and open to the abundance that is all around you. (Pause.)

You are directed to a comfortable chair at the edge of the garden. You inhale deeply and feel even more relaxed. (Pause.) All of your guides and angels are assembled in front of you. Feel their presence as they send you loving energy that clears away any fears, misperceptions, or doubts. You feel free to live the life you came here to live. Your purpose is becoming clear. You feel new hope and courage as you bask in this Divine energy of love.

Do you have any questions? Now is the time to ask. (Pause.) You have only to ask in simple trust and the answers will come; they will always come. Your Divine guidance system is always on and ready to guide you.

Open your eyes when you feel ready, and continue to create the life you came here to live.

Your Intuition Journal

Here you are at the end of the book. It's a great time for a review!

What achievement have you been the most proud of this year?

In what ways have you increased your trust in your intuition?

In what ways have you found it easiest to receive guidance (dreams, inner voice, emotions, meditation, symbolic images, coincidences, and synchronicities)?

What will you do to create even more love, passion, and joy in your life?

If you were your inner guide, what advice would you give yourself about how to live your life?

You have within you the riches of the Universe. Your intuition will always and unwaveringly direct you to love, success, peace, health, and happiness. My wish for you is that you listen to your still, small inner voice and heed its wisdom as it points the way to the life of your dreams.

PRODUCTS AND SERVICES FOR SUCCESS

Lectures and Seminars

Are you looking for a dynamic, inspiring, entertaining, and informative speaker for your next conference or corporate event? Lynn Robinson is one of the nation's leading experts on the topic of intuition. She is also one of the best speakers on the subject. A member of the National Speakers Association with more than fifteen years of speaking experience, Lynn consistently receives rave reviews for the depth of her content, the good-natured, down-to-earth style in which she delivers it, and her winning sense of humor.

Intuitive Consulting for Business

Could your business use an edge? Many business decisions need to be made quickly. Logic and analysis can provide only partial answers, and often there is inadequate data on which to base a decision. Lynn uses her intuition to "tune in" to the core of your business challenge. The information she receives can help you create solutions that enable you to achieve your goals quickly and effectively. Her insights cover a wide spectrum, including creative marketing strategies, ways to build employee motivation, improving the odds on an important sales pitch, and much more.

Audiotapes

Lynn produces a series of guided imagery tapes. Titles include "The Intuitive Life Series," "Prosperity! The Intuitive Path to Creating Abundance," "Creating the Life You Want," and many others.

Free E-mail *Intuition Newsletter*

You'll receive a monthly e-mail digest packed with information you can use, such as valuable tips on how to develop your intuition, book reviews on topics of interest to readers, and intuition and spirituality-related Web links.

Contact Information

Lynn A. Robinson

Intuitive Consulting, Inc.

P. O. Box 81218 • Wellesley Hill, MA 02481 • USA

800-925-4002 or 617-964-0075

E-mail: Lynn@LynnRobinson.com

Web Site: http://www.LynnRobinson.com

ABOUT THE AUTHOR

Lynn Robinson, M.Ed., is one of the nation's leading experts on intuition. She's a popular and widely recognized author and motivational speaker. As an intuition consultant she works with businesses and individuals, offering insights into goals, decisions, and strategies, and teaching the use of intuitive skills for assessing information.

She is the author of four books, including *Divine Intuition: Your Guide to Creating a Life You Love*. It was chosen as one of Amazon.com's "Best of 2001" and was ranked among the top ten books of the year in the Spirituality category. She is also the coauthor of *The Complete Idiot's Guide to Being Psychic*.

Lynn is a columnist and Intuition-at-Work Expert for iVillage.com, a leading destination on the Internet with 9.5 million members. She's been featured in the *Boston Globe* and *USA Today*, and has been a guest on many national radio and television programs on Fox Cable News and the Wisdom Television Network. She's also been interviewed by such publications as the *New York Times*, *Redbook*, *Glamour*, *Good Housekeeping*, *Woman's World*, and *First for Women*.

Lynn teaches that intuition is a ready source of direction available to all of us—an invisible intelligence that animates our world and helps guide our lives. When we follow its wisdom, we are led to success, happiness, peace, and joy. She believes we all have the ability to access this power and develop it for practical use in everyday life as well as for discovering and achieving long-term goals.

She is an active member of the National Speakers Association and a sought-after motivational speaker who helps people make

changes and achieve their goals—both personally and profession-
ally—by following their intuition. With more than fifteen years of
speaking experience, Lynn consistently receives rave reviews for
the depth of her content, the good-natured, down-to-earth style
in which she delivers it, and her winning sense of humor.

Lynn produced the audiotape series *Living the Intuitive Life*, and
authored the popular booklet *Prosperity! The Intuitive Path to Creating
Abundance*. She has been a professional intuitive since 1983 and
is founder and president of Intuitive Consulting, Inc. She pub-
lishes the monthly *Intuition Newsletter* available on her Web site,
www.LynnRobinson.com.